Initials
and
Decorative Alphabets

Initials
and
Decorative Alphabets

Erhardt D. Stiebner
Dieter Urban

Blandford Press
Poole · Dorset

First published in the U.K. in 1985 by
Blandford Press Ltd., Link House,
West Street, Poole, Dorset BH15 1LL

Distributed in the United States by
Sterling Publishing Co., Inc.,
2 Park Avenue, New York, N.Y. 10016

British Library Cataloguing in Publication Data

Stiebner, Erhardt, D.
  Initials and decorative alphabets.
  1. Alphabets
  I. Title   II. Urban, Dieter
  745.6'1   NK3630

ISBN 0 7137 1640 1

Originally published in 1983 as
Initialen und Bildbuchstaben
World copyright © Verlag F. Bruckmann KG,
Munich, Germany.

English translation by Lenore Lengefeld.

Designed and produced by F. Bruckmann KG
Printed and bound in the Federal Republic of Germany.

Contents

On the origin of initials

It was in the fourth century after the birth of Christ that letters marking the beginning of a book, a chapter or a page began to be pronouncedly emphasized and embellished. Size, color and ornamentation were the salient characteristics of such initials. Taken from the Latin "initium" (beginning), this term had something in common with the expressions "initiator" (instigator, originator) and "initiative" (impulse, stimulus).

Initials in the sense of decorative letters were especially cultivated in the early and late Middle Ages. According to their composition, we differentiate between
– initial body (outer form)
– initial ground (inner form) and
– initial foil (background).

In addition to initials composed of the letters themselves and ornamental decoration, calligraphers also developed specimens in which the letter body was replaced by other forms. They used objects or forms which either suggested letters by their intrinsic shape (a man with outstretched arms becomes a "T") or which allowed formation into letters (a snake becomes an "S"). This kind of figure-initial is characteristic of late style epochs, such as the late Romanic and late Gothic eras.

Lettering was employed very early to serve the message of Christ: dissemination of the fixed texts of the evangelists signified to Christianity a competitive battle with the Roman Empire for men's souls. The chirography of the Old and New Testaments, commentaries of church leaders and their theological writings form the major parts of the written testimonies which have come down to us from early Christian times. The manuscripts penned in monasteries were either used directly in religious rites or as study material, as well as for other liturgical needs, like the "missal" (Mass book) or the "psalterium" (hymnbook). They were transcribed and lavishly decorated with ornamentation and figures by dedicated monks. By the close of the first thousand years A. D., the art of creating illuminated manuscripts had developed into one of the most magnificent manifestations of the culture of the Middle Ages. The collections of handwritten books in important cloister libraries, such as those of Neustift near Bressanone in the South Tyrol, Fulda or St. Gallen are not limited to sacred texts, for monasteries in the 13th and 14th centuries were also distinguished scientific research institutes of notable intellectual liberality.

The uncial, developed from the Roman Capitalis and the late Roman Rustica, became the lettering used in early Christian writings. Despite its obvious leanings toward these Roman alphabets, through ascending and descending strokes, as well as initial and ending strokes, it leads to gradual changes in letter forms and thus to the first more readable texts. When the semiuncial appears in the 6th century – written with a half-diagonally cut pen, and whose appearance reminds us more of lowercase than of capital letters – the way is free for the so-called "Caroline minuscule" developed at the close of the 8th century. This is a lowercase lettering based on antique elements which can be written fluidly, thus connecting the individual letters (and requiring clear spacing between words). It provides the impetus for the accentuation of paragraphs and chapter headings.

And this again is the reason for the growing prominence of the initial in the art of making books. It becomes the crowning element in text ornamentation: the more significant the content and purpose of a calligraphic work, the more magnificent its decoration. Originating at the court of Charlemagne, the art of creating religious books begins to spread over Europe about 800 A. D. In the great evangelical works the minuscule dominates: especially important parts of the text were designed with majuscules (capital letters) and chapter headings with splendid initials which often take up an entire page. This is not always a pure decoration; the page-filling initial also fulfills the function of a title page, unknown before the 16th century.

From 1200 on, the round forms of the lowercase letters begin to be modified: lettering becomes more angular, resembling the Gothic pointed arch which is replacing the Roman rounded arch in architecture. 150 years later this process has been completed and ends in "textura". Letters are now completely broken and free of rounded arches. Alphabets are characterized by closely placed vertical elements. This leads to a severe yet expressive, tightly connected script in which initials and other ornamentation stand out with great effectiveness.

After the invention of the printing press in 1453, when Johannes Gutenberg first made possible the reproduction of a message, the heyday of hand-painted initials was over. The unsystematic – since uniquely created – decorative letter had to make way for the printed initial. By the end of the 15th century, whole alphabets had already been systemized.

Initials in the eras of late antiquity

In the second century, books made of folded and bound leaves replaced the papyrus rolls of the ancient world: the skins of cattle or sheep were cured to make parchment and inscribed with the juice of gallnut (the expression, "That can't be put onto cowhide" – It's beyond belief! – probably originated here). One sheepskin provided the material for a book page of about the dimensions of today's DIN A2 size. Each step of this process – from tanning to writing to decorating and illustrating – was done by hand, always resulting in an original, even if another handwriting was copied.

In "Initialen aus großen Handschriften" (Initials from Great Manuscripts) by J. J. G. Alexander, one can read that... "the early decorative letters must be examined in relation to the epoch in which they originated and in relation to their purpose." An excellent study by Carl Nordenfalk on the earliest initials appeared in 1970, entitled "Die spätantiken Zierbuchstaben" (Decorative Lettering in Late Antiquity). In this work he stated that there are two determining factors in the creation and development of decorative initials. The first one arises from a changed attitude toward the text: "In ancient times, literature was understood as something spoken or listened to, since stories were always declaimed. This meant that literature related to speech or hearing, but not to seeing. However, when man began to understand texts as something visually conveyed through the written word – a development that surely contributed to the dissemination and triumph of Christianity with its emphasis on the revelations of the written words of the Bible – this external visual identity had of necessity to become the object of design. Texts could now be decor-

Initials from a German Bible, 10th cn.

Byzantine, 12th cn.

ated and embellished, while up to that time only simple textual arrangements, diagrams and illustrations necessary for better understanding and clarification of the text were thought fitting."

The second factor relates to the class of persons who were assigned the task of reading and writing in ancient times. "It was usually slaves who did the copying and reciting. It was only when the owner of the book also became its reader and/or its creator (the two could naturally be identical) – a relatively free artisan – that the independence necessary for a real interest in text decoration was present."

Even before the rise of Christianity, Roman handwritten books were often illustrated and decorated. The oldest surviving initials are to be found in an excerpt of Virgil's writings dating from the end of the 4th century. These initials serve not only to separate the strophes, but also introduce a line of verse placed on the upper end of each page. This means that the manuscript must have had as many initials as it did pages – probably 657, of which unfortunately only seven have survived.

The decorative initial as we know it, and as it found expression in Western European book art had its beginnings in the Celtic-Germanic domain. Yet this does not mean that the influences of the eras of late antiquity or of the Byzantine era were not to be found in the first creations of Western European writers.

Nevertheless it is the artistic character of Teutons and Celts, that is, western writers, which is so clearly observable in this genre. It is dynamic, filled with an irrepressible joy in ornamentation – totally different from the harmonious proportions and classical forms of the book art of late antiquity.

11

In the pictorial motifs of this initial ornamentation, which reached its culmination from the 8th to the 11th century in Irish/Anglo-Saxon book art, art motifs of late antiquity such as meanders, palmettes, bird, fish and dragon monstrosities and also human and animal figures alternate with highly original ornaments of Celtic-Germanic origin. The motifs are involuted and inextricably entwined without beginning or end. In this severely linear book ornamentation, a new design principle is manifested which unites classical Roman order with emotionally charged Celtic dynamism and energy.

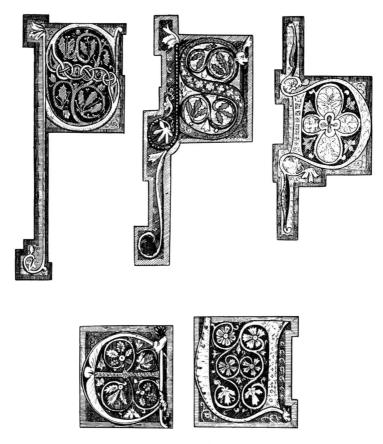

France, 13th cn.

12

Irish/Anglo-Saxon book art

Hundreds of years before the civilization of Western Europe, Celts had colonized an area stretching from Spain to Hungary, including southern Germany, France, northern Italy and even reaching into Asia Minor. They were ousted from some of their settlements by the Teutons, and conquered and assimilated by the Romans in Gaul and Britain. In the wake of the Romans came the Christians, whose missionary work was especially effective in Ireland. Irish monks preserved native literature in handwritten manuscripts, and it was they who brought the art of making books to the European continent and founded the first monasteries in the era to which we owe the first decorative initials. The fact that this new art was soon taken over by Anglo-Saxon and Teutonic monks does not lessen the significance of the immense accomplishments of these first monasteries with their calligraphic workshops, masters and apprentices.

The Irish influence on book art, first in England and then in Middle Europe can be followed in the "Book of Kells", a gospel book created in Scotland about 700. Irish monks in flight from invading Vikings brought this book to Kells in the earldom of Meath in Ireland, and it is still preserved in Trinity College Library in Dublin.
The Irish played a major role in the conversion of the Anglo-Saxons to Christianity. This was achieved with artistically created manuscripts containing unique intertwined initials – possibly the most fantastic and complex in existence.
They are decorated with abstract ornaments such as dotted lines, spirals and bands, but most impressive of all are the many stylized, often acutely observed illustrations of human figures and animals to be found in text pages; nature studies in sacred writings – even though not a central feature of the overall design – are to develop into a typical characteristic of Gothic book art.

In the "Book of Lindisfarne", created about 700 in Anglo-Saxon Northumbria, initials are also covered with ornamentation, yet the spatial context is not particularly well-designed. Here a more pronounced feeling for book page design can already be observed, and ornaments no longer overflow in all directions.

Book illumination
in the Carolingian Renaissance

In contrast to Irish and Merovingian chirographies, manuscripts in the Carolingian era were commissioned by great patrons: the "Ebo-Evangelarium", the "Drogo-Sacramental" and the bibles of Charles II are all associated with the great personages at whose behest these costly gospel books were created. Charlemagne was the first to erect court schools where scribes and illuminators worked together to supply a reawakened interest in antiquity with manuscripts featuring antiqua initials and miniatures in classical form. Ornamentation now becomes finer; figures are no longer a part of the design as in Irish/Anglo-Saxon chirography, but are usually set before a unicolored background. In the severe surface style of the Carolingian codices, particularly in the late 9th century, Celtic plaited and animal ornamentation seems to be tamed, supplanted by classical motifs such as the acanthus and palmettes. For the decoration of initials and title pages, in addition to yellow, green and blue tones, red (minium = lead oxide) and gold are now employed.

Some of the most important sites in the development of Carolingian book illumination were (in addition to the great monasteries of northern France):

– The monastery of St. Gallen, founded by the Irish monk Gallus. At first fully under Irish influence, the Teutonic element slowly gained sway (borders and intertwined band ornamentation based on classical tendril motifs, gold with sporadic touches of silver, colored backgrounds, sometimes in sienna, green or blue). Typical of the general development of this style was the era between the 8th and 12th centuries. The crowning achievement of book art of this period was the "Folchard-Psalter" and the "Golden Psalter". Dur-

Initials by Antoine Vérard. France 15th cn.

Cologne, 16th cn., after an alphabet by Albrecht Dürer

ing the Ottonian era, the center of book design moved to the neighboring

– Reichenau monastery, where further stylistic changes occurred, especially in the naturalness of flower illustrations and in motifs taken from older paintings. One major change consisted of using the "punches" (spaces within letters) for illustrations, which meant that the initial became the frame for a picture.

At the time that the Ottonians came to power, the Romanic style had already reached its full development. The Carolingian style, with its simplicity and classical severity, made way for a more natural one. The intertwined motif, the initial filled with lively movement, the adorned flourishes and curlicues – all of these reached their fullest flowering. The initial was gradually replaced by the illustration.

In Gothic book art, the decorative initial was now only a form, no longer content plus form – only a lovely decoration and nothing more; gold disappeared from the curlicues and became a flat background, as did coloration. Initials placed before a plain background characterized the design of this period for some time. Naturally depicted flower and landscape motifs alternated with severe, abstract illustrations. The great era of hand-illuminated initials was over, and the era of printing in the not-too-distant future.

Initial art in early printed works

Since illuminators relinquished very reluctantly the handwritten book with which they were associated for so long, their illuminated initials survived for a time in unbroken tradition in early printed works. As a sort of obeisance to conservative tastes and ideas about how a beautiful book should look, the art of illuminators and "rubricators" (painters of red tints) lived on for several generations: in the incunabula, printers left spaces free for decorative initials, which were then painted in by illuminators to achieve the same artistic effect as in a handwritten manuscript. The late Gothic era saw ornamentation in the inner spaces of large initials increasingly supplanted by finely painted depictions of figures relating to the textual content, thus making it easier for the reader to understand. In increasing numbers, letters for initials were made from metal or wood, then set into page headings instead of the previously hand-painted initials. The first initials printed in a single process are to be found in the "Psalter Printing", created by Fust and Schöffer in 1457. This also marks the first successful attempt to print multi-color (red and blue) initials. Although Gutenberg tried for some time to copy as exactly as possible the chirography of the Middle Ages in its lettering forms and decorative initials, this idea was soon abandoned as time-consuming and too expensive. Around the year 1480 we find the book becoming a utilitarian object, and in letterpress composition, the letter is developed into an established typographical unit.

For some time to come, the production of initials occurs in many places on parallel lines: many of the early, usually woodcut initials seem only to serve as a frame for hand-coloring. On the other hand, in Augsburg one of the first printers, Erhard Ratdolt, experimented with color printing, although without making use of the expensive and rather unpractical method of two-color psalter initials (one which is unique in the history of printing art). Ratdolt's technique was to print uppercase letters in a different color. With this process, together with his marvelous initial designs, he achieved splendid effects.

The first designs cut in metal were modelled on lettering of the Romanic epoch; these were then colored and ornamented by hand. Since their black/white printing appeared somewhat meager, this limitation led to initial forms in strong black/white contrasts and accentuated designs. Cutting techniques in wood and metal also exerted an influence on the form of decorative lettering. In this way the classical

Netherlands (?), middle of the 17th cn.

Renaissance initials were created, usually negative white on a black background and richly ornamented after patterns of antiquity with masks, vases, cherubs, grotesqueries, beasts and flowers, nude human figures and mythical-allegorical figures intertwined with plantlike tendrils. These motifs can be found in the works of Italian printers (Venetian, for instance), as well as in those of German woodcarvers who illustrated books, such as Albrecht Dürer (see ill.). About the middle of the 16th century, the so-called "form-cutters" in the Germanic lands had reached the peak of perfection in the production of woodcut alphabets.

Letter "Q" from a 16th cn. alphabet,
Paris or Lyon

Decline in the 17th and 18th centuries

At the beginning of the 16th century, when France rose to become the leading arbiter of culture, initial plates were already being produced which were cast with matrices. This production method was probably originated by Claude Garamond, the first independent type foundryman of that age. Up to about 1500, the printer also had to be die-cutter, type foundryman, woodcarver and publisher in one person. Now the economic division of labor made these various activities into independent professions. Calligraphers, excluded from the production of books by this development, turned more and more to writing for commercial enterprises. As writing masters they created numerous specimens for gothic and schwabacher initials, which, however, were seldom used for printed texts. Their designs, including elements of Islamic ornaments such as arabesque and mauresque, have been handed down to us today in the form of specimen books. Up to the close of the 16th century, these books contained initial designs for the woodcarving process which was later supplanted by copperplate engraving.

This changeover came at the same time that writing with a broad penstroke gave way to the so-called chancery hand, in which a sharply pointed, deeply notched and more flexible quill was used.

Printed initials in the 17th and 18th centuries were mainly engravings, in spite of the fact that this process involved an exact register in a second pressrun. Strongly influenced by copperplate engraving, decorative initials in the rococo era of the 18th century are adorned with exuberant curves and delicate leaf and flower ornamentation. At the same time, italic initials now gain in importance. A novelty gains popularity: quick-change frames and borders can be designed from single decorative elements and letters can be exchanged as needed.

About the middle of the 18th century, three renowned printers created type faces that are still in the forefront of typography today: Baskerville in England, Bodoni in Italy and Didot in France. With the exception of Bodoni, which features classicistic engraved initials, most other printers rejected any sort of book decoration and strove to emulate classical models of antiquity. Instead of the initial, somewhat larger capital letters now dominate body types without detracting from the severe typographical design.

From a manuscript in St. Geneviève monastery,
Paris, 18th cn.

Diversity of styles in the 19th century

The initial of the 19th century is really the initial of the Victorian age: England enjoyed the results of the industrial revolution to a degree that put its development far ahead of other countries – in the field of typography as well. Since English products, English know-how and English style were dominant all over the world, it was no wonder that the continent and above all North America fell greatly under its influence. "American types" of the late 19th century were mainly borrowed from English specimens and also from type foundries on the continent (see ill.).

At the beginning of the 19th century, the art of the initial had already begun a new flowering. Illustrative solutions are popular in which the letter is set into a scenic vignette or formed out of various figures or objects. Litho etching, invented in 1798 by Alois Senefelder, has been added to the prevailing techniques of woodcut and copperplate engraving. Previously unknown design possibilities are now achievable with this new technique.

The calligraphy masters of the Middle Ages were the spiritual forefathers of the lettering lithographers of the 19th century. Their creations with pen and diamond-pointed stone-engraving stylus featured initials made up of human figures, beasts, plants and architectural details. They were technically perfect, original and imaginative, yet as time went on, they were less and less convincing on an artistic and aesthetic level.

Reproduction of Plantin initials (16th cn.) by Thomas Cleland, 20th cn.

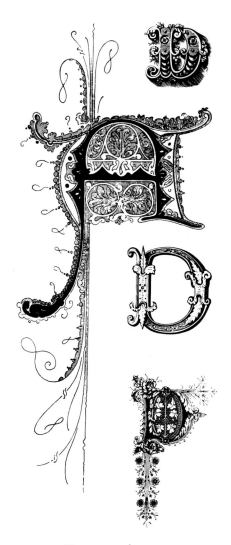

From top to bottom:
Italy, 19th cn.; Germany, 19th cn.;
England, 19th cn.; USA, 19th cn.

New impulses in the 20th century

One exception to this was William Morris (1834–1896), one of the most versatile English craftsmen and book artists, whose work was linked to socio-political reforms. As a passionate opponent of industrialization and the decline of taste which accompanies it, his main efforts were against the mass production of art and for the revival of craftsmanship. His orientation was toward Gothic style in that period when art and craftsmanship were still undivided. With his designs of wallpaper, furniture and utensils of every kind, and with his extremely ornamental designs of books and bindings, Morris exerted a strong influence on Art Nouveau. His decorative initials, usually adorned with flower motifs, and his pictorial alphabets from the period between 1895 and 1905 may be described as the successful attempt at setting an art trend whose goal was nothing less than the complete alteration of life styles. Associated with the revival of typography in Germany were names such as Peter Behrens, Heinrich Vogeler and Otto Eckmann. The latter is known as one of the most important typographers of the Art Nouveau movement, and his "Eckmann type face" was the most popular of its period. The further development of this art trend was disrupted by the First World War and its subsequent effect on art and the economy.

During the twenties, a period that was characterized by the theories of functionalism, lettering and type were also ruled by design principles which embodied mathematical precision and sober objectivity. Any kind of adornment was rejected. Yet during this period there were many artists who rebelled against the norm of prosaism and included decorative elements in their book designs, although in a more severe mode than that of Art Nouveau.

It may be generally stated that since the middle of the twentieth century, the decorative initial has once again become popular. Again it serves as the frame for an image or is surrounded by a scene, as our specimen of the work of the American John Cleland shows (see ill.). This artist also models his designs on motifs from early handwritten manuscripts.

Whether or not the great tradition of the initial will be continued in the late 20th century still remains to be seen. Modern technologies such as photocomposition with its letter modifications or the invention of rub-on lettering will probably not serve to improve matters in this direction. On the other hand, impulses from the USA, awakening to new life a wealth of Anglo-American types from the Victorian era, have significantly widened the supply of initial specimens. In the wake of the nostalgia wave of the seventies, a revival of 19th century and Art Nouveau initials has taken place. Added to these activities are the new and individual, but often questionable lettering creations which are coming onto the market. These often unite the most disparate styles; they are passing fads, original or avant-garde, yet numbering among them works of fine illustration and inventive fantasy.

The last section of illustrations features experimental works: young designers from two German art schools have created contemporary variations on the "pictorial initial". In these designs can be read the entire range of the above-mentioned trends.

Initials by Otto Eckmann for "Pan" magazine, 1896

Alphabet by Peter Behrens, 1908 ▷

25

Initials by Curt Reibetanz, 1925

Contemporary decorative initials   (p. 322–333)

In the introduction, we spoke of the flowering of painted initials at the beginning of our second thousand years of Christianity. Decorative initials of that time were first composed of borders, entwined bands and classical tendril motifs. Naturally depicted flower motifs and revivals from the 8th and 9th centuries were later added: children, cherubs and also animals and nature studies. The first initials cut in wood in the 15th century took their subjects from handwritten manuscripts. Early printers inserted these additional letters into their printing forms after they finally found it too troublesome and expensive to fill the spaces left in the first books with handpainted initials. If this kind of decorative initial was not composed of ornamentation, but of figures, it became a pictorial letter or even a whole alphabet, but it was almost always used as an initial.

Studies from the Westend Art School,
Frankfurt on Main, Germany, 1983

27

Today pictorial letters are primarily applied as an attractive eye-catching element on book or record covers, or in posters, seldom as initials. They are often used as a pictorial motif to represent a certain concept, that is, not the letter as image but the other way around. And this is the way we should look at the lettering variations created by students at the Academy of Fine Arts in Braunschweig (Hochschule für Bildende Künste). For this project, a guideline system was developed at the school in which relationships between form and content were set down.

When a design student is confronted with the theme, »pictorial letters«, and he may choose any letters between A and Z for a specific concept, he will probably try – aside from the techniques involved – to illustrate his »favorite image«. This results in widely differing interpretations: »A« may stand for »Aal« (eel) to someone, where someone else sees a parrot (»Ara«). Those more interested in botany will decide for »Agave« or »Ast« (branch)...

On the other hand, the goals of the design project at the Westend School of Art in Frankfurt were to translate the chosen term into a generally understandable image and to depict the individual letter or word in a witty and visually attractive manner.

Letter "S" from a cartoon-alphabet
of Günter Hugo Magnus, Germany

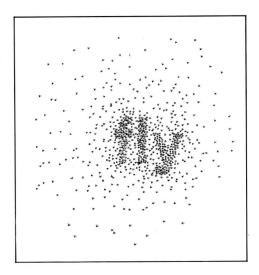

The word "fly" made of flies,
College of Art, Darmstadt

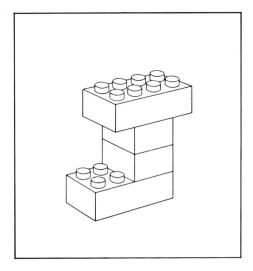

Letter "J"
made of game bricks

Illustrations

Initials from early Irish manuscripts, 8th cn.

INCPT
LIBER
NVM̄Rɪ

CATUSQUEESIDNS
ADMOYSENINDE
SERTOSYNAJINIA
BERNACULOFOE
DERIS·PRIMADIE

EZRAE

NANNOPRI
MOCYRIRE
CISPERSA
RUM UTIM
PLERCTUR
UERBUDNI
EXOREHIERI
MIAESUSCI
TAUITDN̄S
SPM̄CYRIRE
CISPERSARŪ
ETTRANSDU
XIIUOCÉIN
UNIUERSO
RECNOSUO
ETIAMPER
SCRIPTURĀ
DICENS

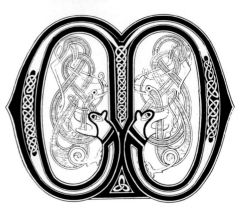

Initials from early Irish manuscripts, 8th cn.

CXLCTXR

meosculooris

Initials from the second Bible of Charles II, after 865 A. D.

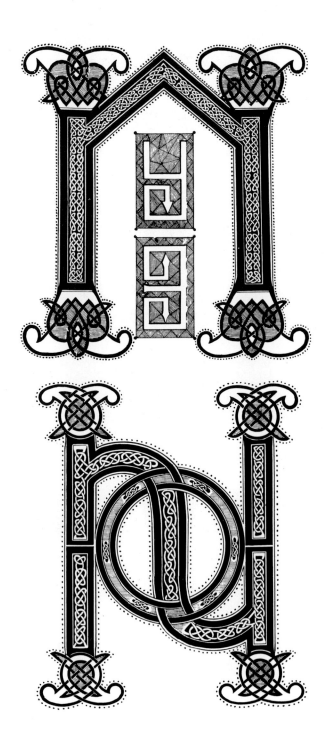

Initials from the second Bible of Charles II, after 865 A. D.

B

M

O

Byzantine, 12th cn.

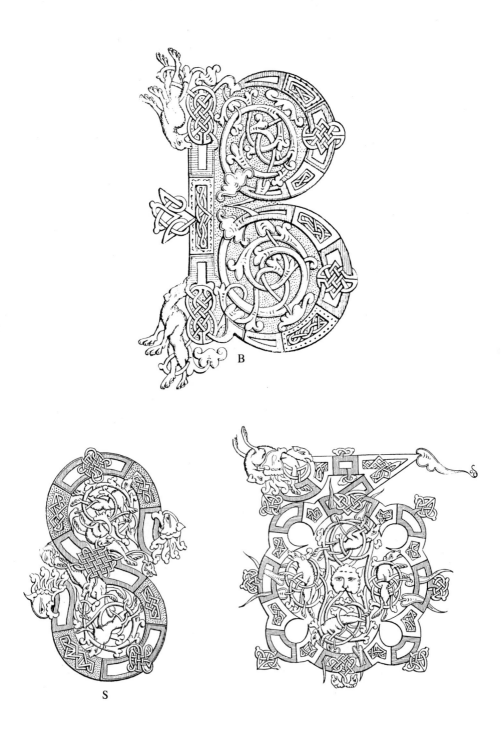

B

S

Byzantine, 12th cn.

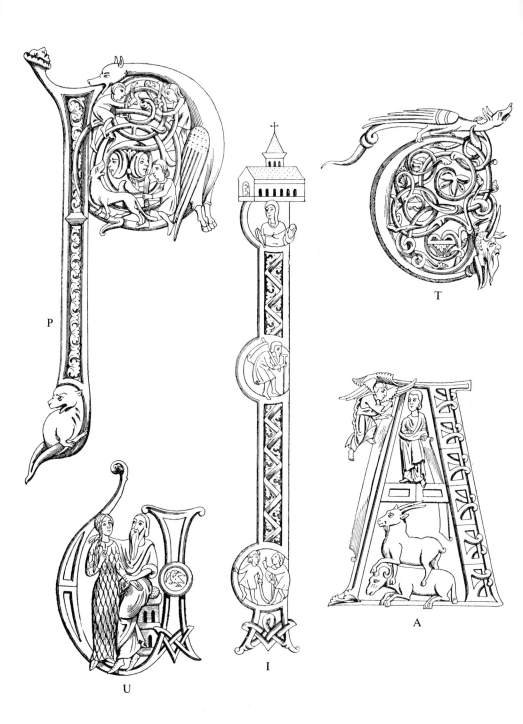

P

T

U

I

A

France, 12th cn.

P

H

France, 12th cn.

39

C

C

U

T

France, 13th cn.

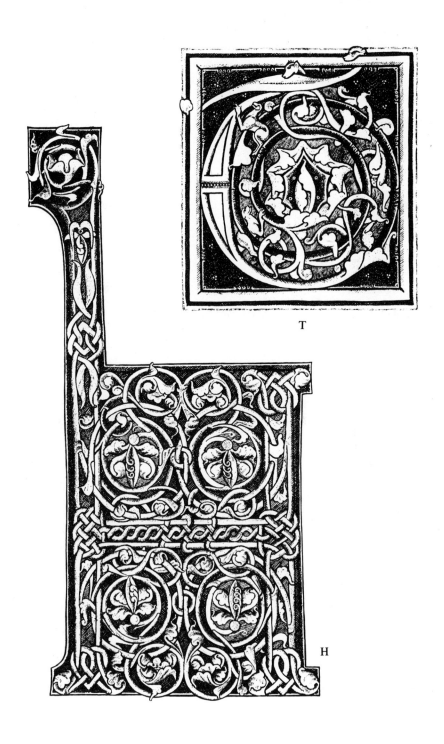

T

H

France, 13th cn.

Line initials from 12th century manuscripts

QVSE·TTAQ;

CX OZ· EZEC

Line initials from 12th century manuscripts

Romanesque initial, 12th cn.

Romanesque initials, 12th cn.

German and french areas, 11th, 12th, 13th cn.

Letters in various colors from manuscripts, 12th cn.

Simple initials, colors were generally gold, red, blue, green. 12th cn.

From manuscripts in the British museum, 14th cn.

Finicky sort of work in late manuscripts, 14th cn.

From a Missal in the Vatican Library. Italy, 14th cn.

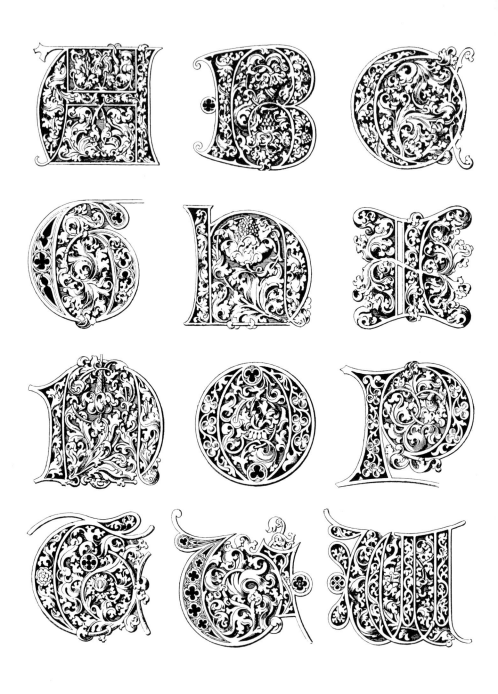

Italy, 14th cn.

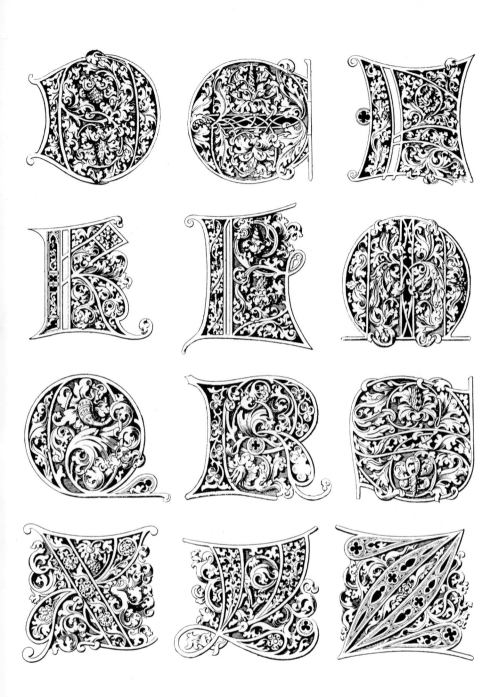

Italy, 14th cn.

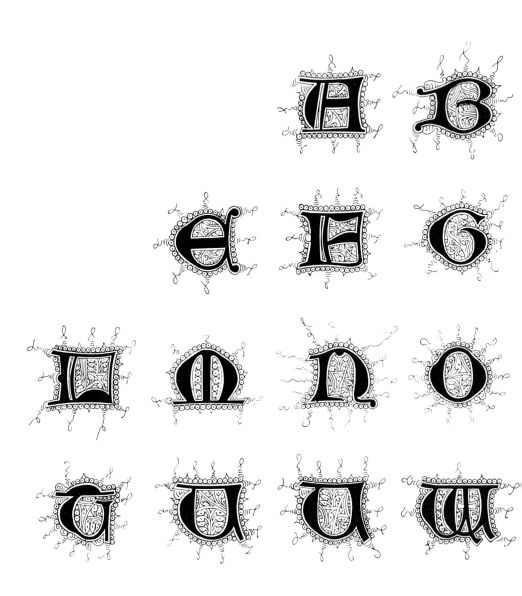

Germany, 14th cn.

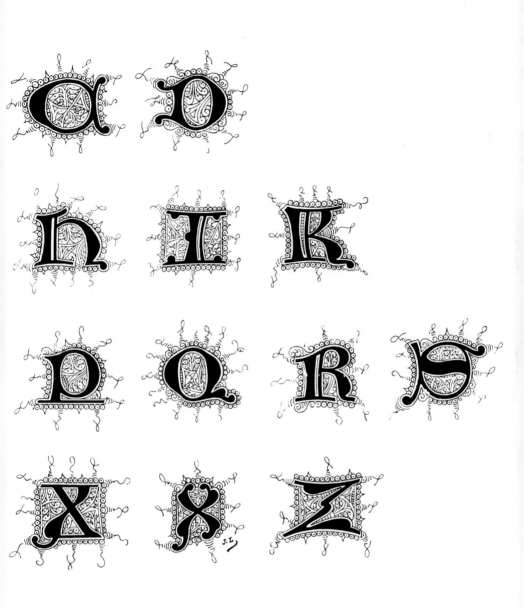

Germany, 14th cn.

From a German Bible printed in Nuremberg by Johann Sensenschmidt, 15th cn.

From a German Bible printed by Günther Zainer, Augsburg, 15th cn.

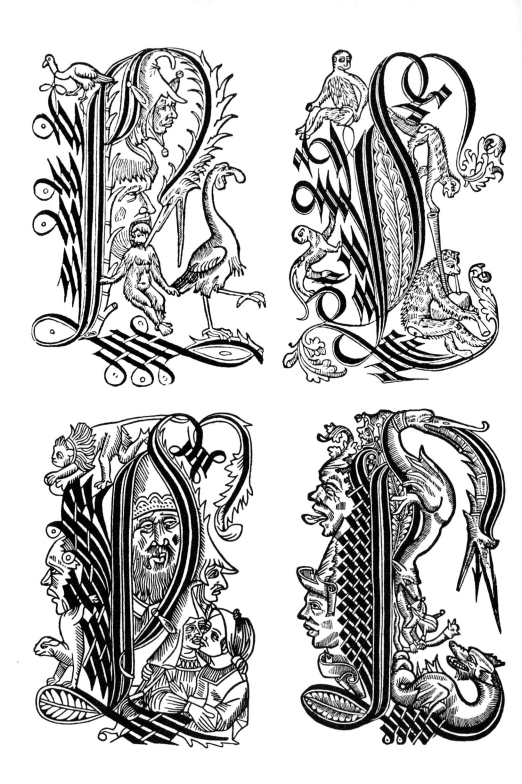

France, late 15th cn.

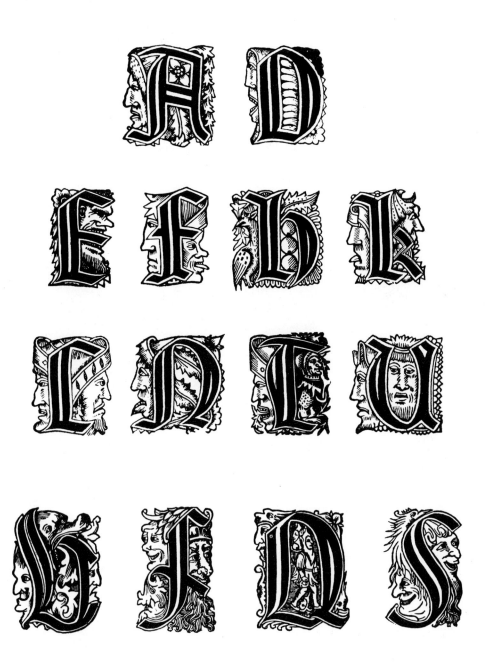

France. Lecoq, 15th cn.

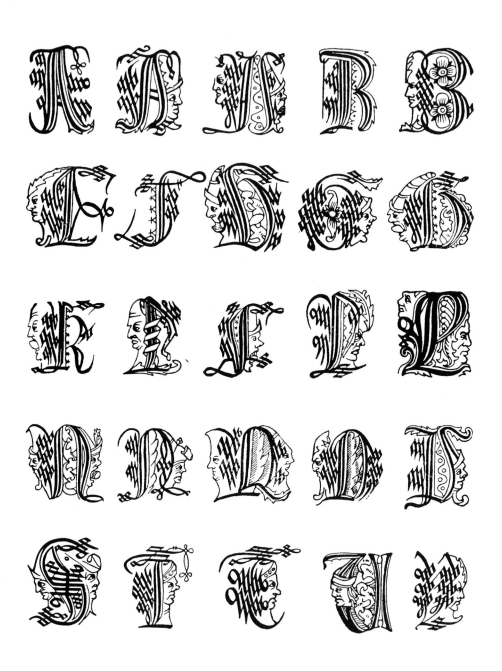

France. Antoine Vérard, 15th cn.

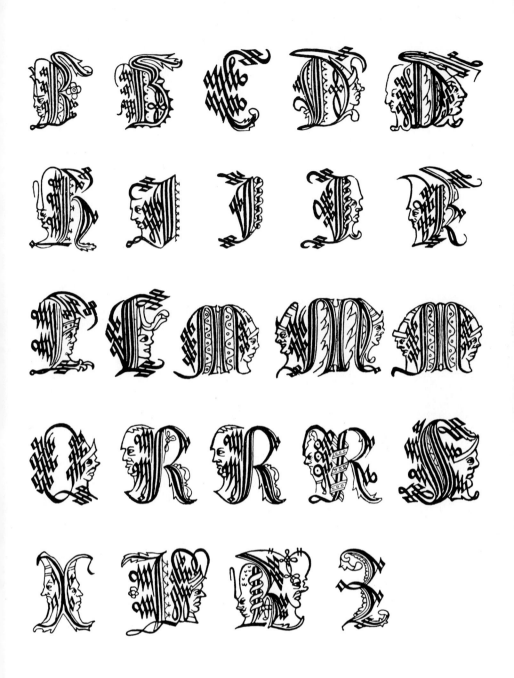

France. Antoine Vérard, 15th cn.

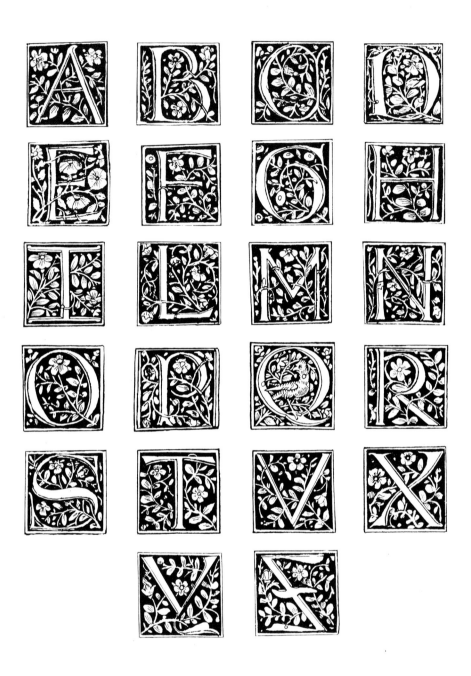

France. Printed by Le Masson & Co, 15th cn.

France, 15th cn.

Burlesque alphabet by Master E. S., about 1460

Burlesque alphabet by Master E. S., about 1460

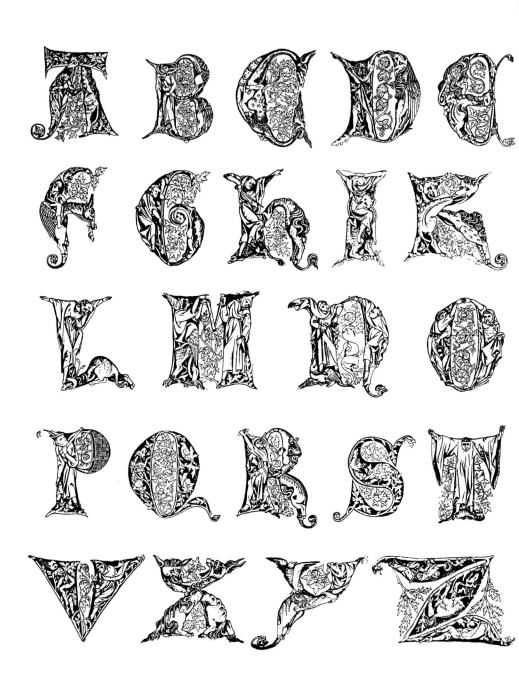

Germany (?), late 15th cn.

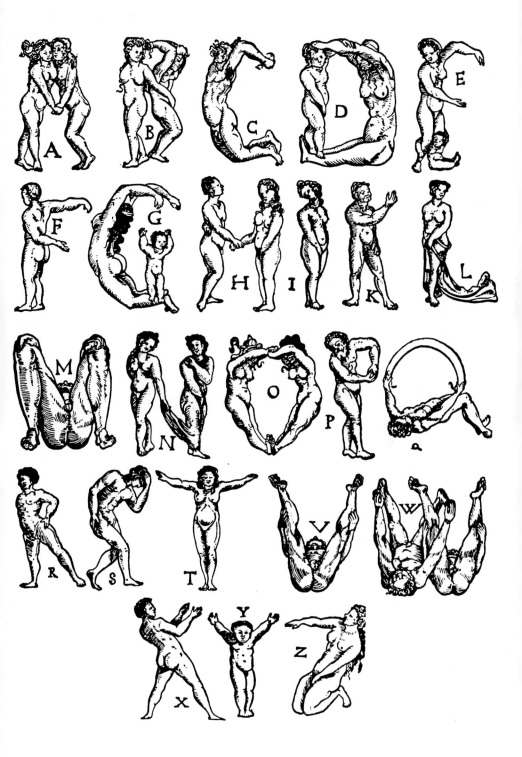

Human figure alphabet. Germany (?), 16th cn.

Top: From a geographic essay by Zacharius Lilius, printed in Venice, 15th cn.
Bottom: Printed in Cologne by Melchior Novesianus, 15th cn.

Top: France, 15th and 16th cn. Bottom: Germany, 16th cn.

Decorative initials from the workshop of Peter Lichtenstein and the brothers Veneti

France, 15th cn.

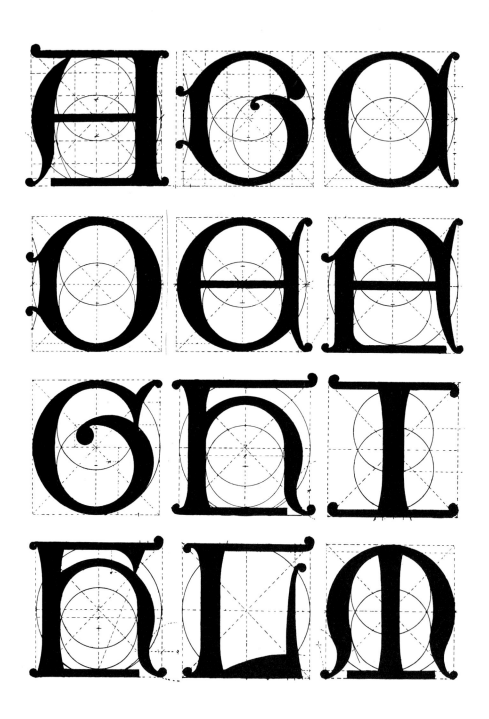

Constructed initials, 15th cn.

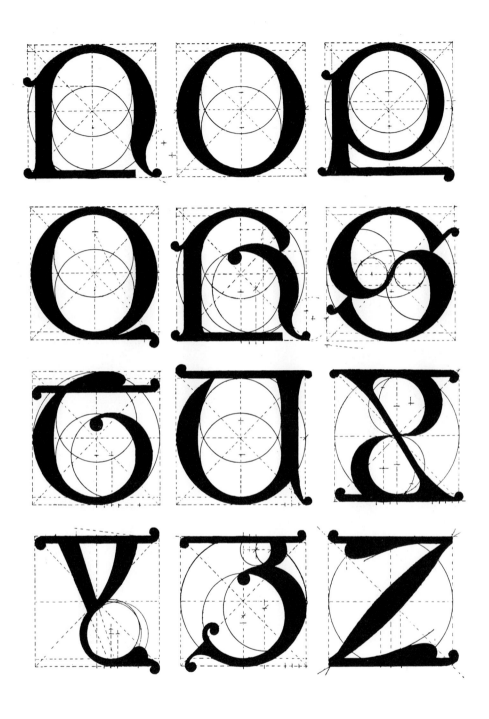

Constructed initials, 15th cn.

Gothic letters, 15th cn.

Gothic letters, 15th cn.

Decorative letters from diverse German workshops, 15th/16th cn.

Decorative letters from diverse German workshops, 15th/16th cn.

Initials taken from a copy of the "Roman de la rose", beginning of the 16th cn.

Initials taken from a copy of the "Roman de la rose", beginning of the 16th cn.

AD REVEREN

DISS. IN CHRISTO PATREM ILLVSTRISS
PRINCIPEM ALBERTVM BRANDEN
burgeñ.Cardinalem Archiepiſcopum Moguntiñ.& Magde-
burgeñ.Principem electorem,primatemꝗ̃,VLRICHI
Hutteni Equ.in Titum Liuium hiſtoricum,libris
auctum duobus,Præfatio.

 VCTVS NVPER, RECVPERA-
ta quadam minime contemnenda ſui parte T.
Liuius,cum ſecum ipſe conſultaret, ubi, & cuius
ſub inſcriptione in lucem exiret,hanc noſtram ſibi delegit auream Moguntiam,pater ac princeps
colendiſſime, inter alias Europæ urbes digniſſi-
mā ratus arbitror, ubi renaſci gauderet, tuáque
perſpecta ingēti erga ſtudioſos ac literatos omes
benignitate, aptū ſe inueniſſe putauit principē,
cuius auſpícijs prodire in publicum, ac mūdo ſe
oſtēdere uellet. Ille ſcilicet aut cogitauit hæc, aut
non inepte à nobis cogitaſſe putari debet.Nam ſi uel locū uoluit Liuius ali-
quem ſuo decorare egreſſu, quem debuit urbi, artis omnium quæ uſquam
ſunt,aut unquam fuerunt præſtantiſſimæ inuētrici,ac alumnæ(impreſſorſā
puto,quam hæc dedit)præferreʔ Vel hominem deligere ſibi, cuius impreſ-
ſum fronti ſuæ nomen,ueluti temporis monetam,quoquo ire contingat, ho-
noris cauſſa præferret, alium certe maluiſſe neminē crediderimus quàm te,
cuius in euehendis literarum ſtudijs, ac augendo optimarum diſciplinarum
cultu,incredibilis ardor ac mira induſtria, in percolendis uero doctis homi-
nibus immēſa liberalitas ac regia plane munificētia.Hæc efficiunt,ut omnes
quotquot ſumus aut hominum opinione docti, aut re uera recte ſtudioſi,
ad unum hoc quoddam uelut aſylum confugiamus, quanquam tu nō ſuſtines confugientes nos, uerū cunctantes ad te ultro rapis. Poſſem hic referre,
quos uiros,quàm tu familiariter accerſiueris,quæ dona alijs dederis,quanta
multis pollicitus ſis, quomodo pecunia pariter ac dignitate nonnullos au-
xeris,& tua aula ut aperta ſit doctis hoſpitaliſſime uiris, niſi ſcirem multum
à tua alienum eſſe modeſtia,in Liuij præfatione tuarū tibi laudum encomiū
legi.Certe profecto & locus eſt opportunus hic,ubi non renaſci tantum uelit
eximius ſcriptor, ſed oriri etiam olim potuerit, & tu dignus, qui patronum
in uulgo Liuij agas.Neꝗ uiciſſim (ut tua fretus bonitate dicā aliquid libere)
indignus ille qui tibi offeratur,tibiꝗ̃ dedicetur, ac tuo qui prætento nomine
in manibus habeatur. Quinetiā ſi liberius adhuc audire me ſuſtines, dicam

a ij non

Border in cut metal. From the workshop of Johann Schöffer, Mainz, 1518

Decorative initials in roman type, 16th cn.

Gothic initials, 15th cn.

Renaissance initials, beginning of the 16th cn.

Workshop of Lufft, Wittenberg. Design of Lucas Cranach, 1512

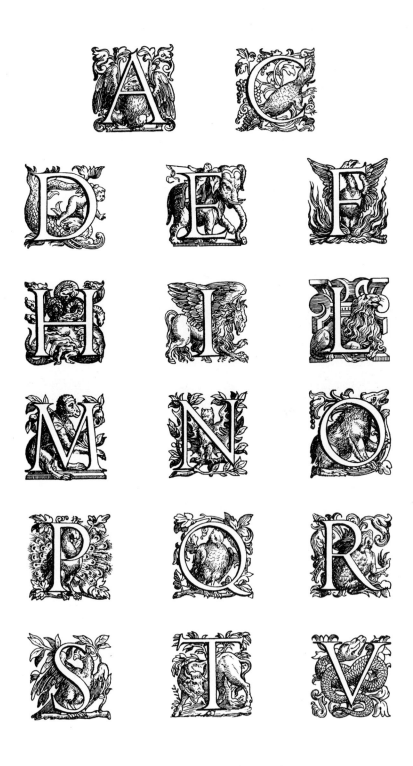

Venice, by the Aldi brothers, 16th cn.

France, 16th cn.

Germany, Jean Knoblauk, 16th cn.

Letter H by Melchior Novesianus. Workshop of Quentell, ca. 1535

Alphabet from the workshop of Eucharius Hirtzhorn, Cologne. After Albrecht Dürer, about 1524

Alphabet from the workshop of Eucharius Hirtzhorn, Cologne. After Albrecht Dürer, about 1524

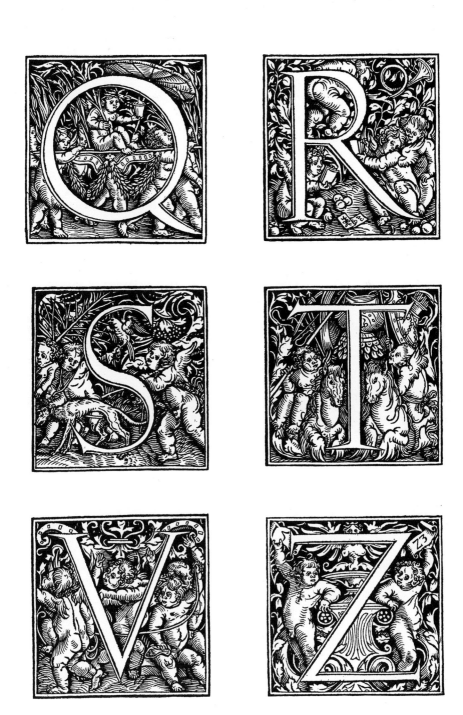

Alphabet from the workshop of Eucharius Hirtzhorn, Cologne. After Albrecht Dürer, about 1524

France, 16th cn.

France, 16th cn.

Printed in Orleans by Pierre de la Rouière, 16th cn.

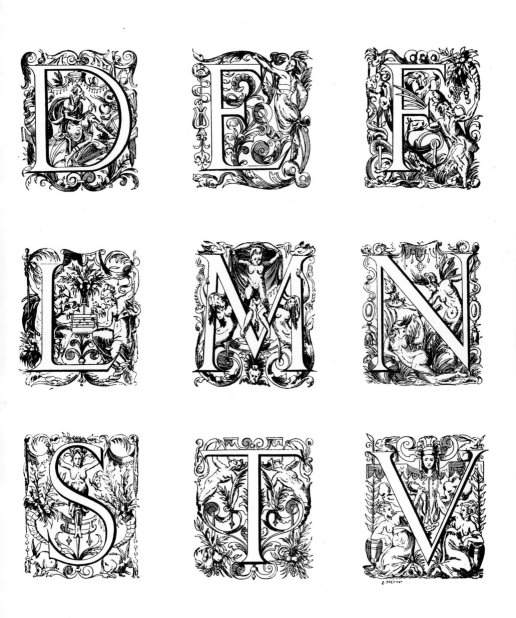

Printed in Orleans by Pierre de la Rouière, 16th cn.

Initials by Hans Holbein, used by Valentin Curio, Basel, 1522

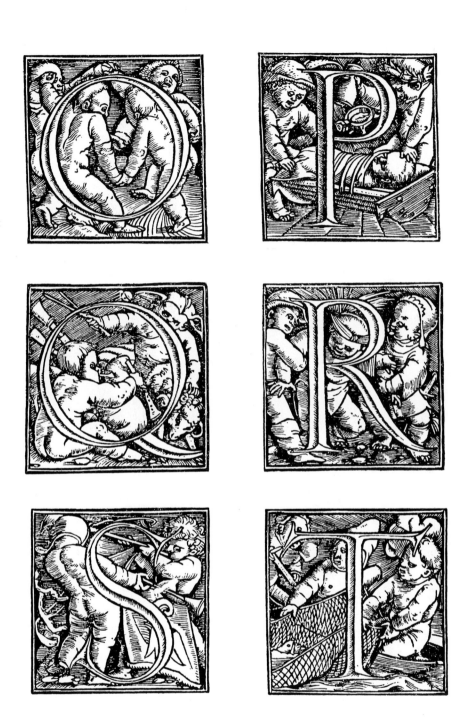

Initials by Hans Holbein, used by Valentin Curio, Basel, 1522

Venice, 16th cn.

Workshop of Johann Schöffer, Mainz, 1518

France, 16th cn.

France, 16th cn.

Johann Theodor de Bry, "Neues künstlerisches Alphabet", Frankfurt am Main, 1595

Johann Theodor de Bry, "Neues künstlerisches Alphabet", Frankfurt am Main, 1595

Johann Theodor de Bry, "Neues künstlerisches Alphabet", Frankfurt am Main, 1595

Johann Theodor de Bry, "Neues künstlerisches Alphabet", Frankfurt am Main, 1595

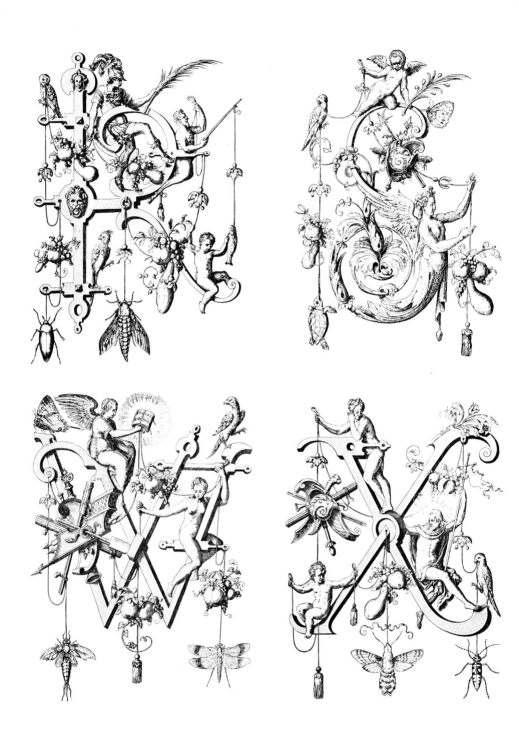

Johann Theodor de Bry, "Neues künstlerisches Alphabet", Frankfurt am Main, 1595

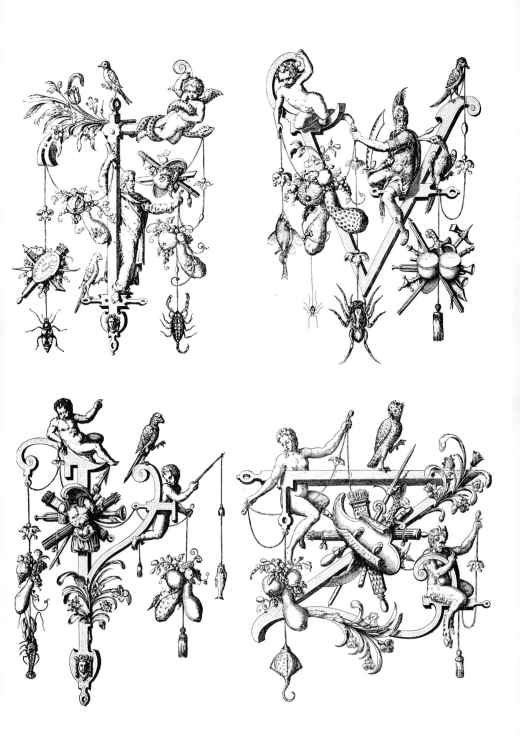

Johann Theodor de Bry, "Neues künstlerisches Alphabet", Frankfurt am Main, 1595

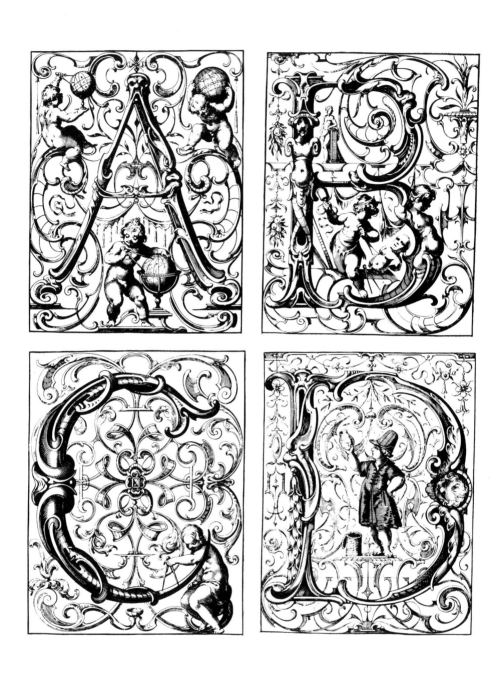

Netherlands (?), middle of the 17th cn.

Netherlands (?), middle of the 17th cn.

Urban Wyss, "Ein Neuw Fundamentbuch". Zurich, 1562

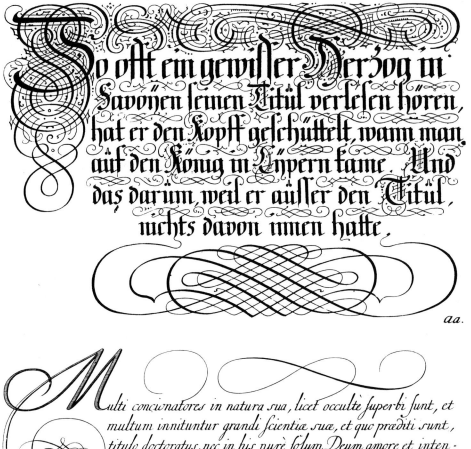

So offt ein gewiſſer Herzog in
Savoyen ſeinen Titul verleſen hören,
hat er den Kopff geſchüttelt, wann man
auf den König in Cypern kame. Und
das darum, weil er auſſer den Titul,
nichts davon innen hatte.

aa.

*Multi concionatores in natura sua, licet occulte superbi sunt, et
multum innituntur grandi scientiæ suæ, et quo præditi sunt,
titulo doctoratus, nec in his pure solum Deum amore et inten-
tione prosequuntur, nec ejus duntaxat gloriam in literarum
studio spectant, sed seipsos plus satis quaerunt et amant,
hosque ita litera occidit. Cum enim vas eorum inane et feru-
lentum sit, merum ideoq coelestis doctrinæ, licet purissimæ
et optimae, per illud transiens, anima munda Deum amanti
et intendenti, insipidum fit, gratiamque non adfert.*

Mm.

Michael Baurenfeind, "Der Schreibkunst vollkommener Wiederherstellung anderer Teil".
Nuremberg, 1736

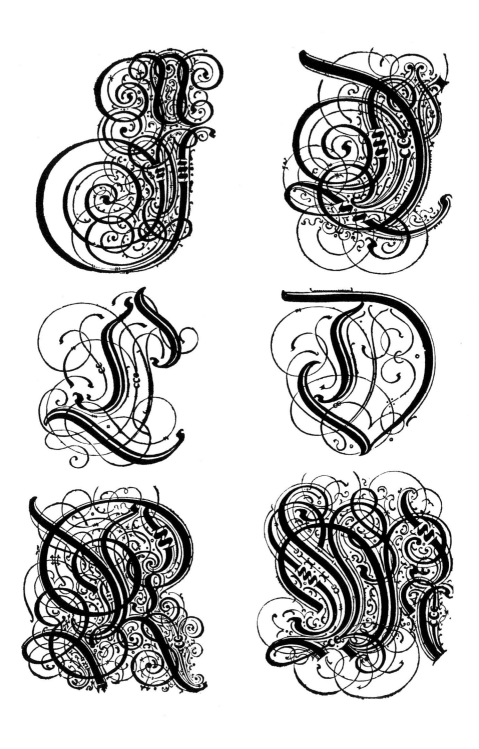

Baroque initials, 17th cn.

Baroque initials, 17th cn.

Baroque initials, 17th cn.

Paul Frank, letter T from "Schatzkammer allerhand Versalien Lateinisch und Deutsch".
Nuremberg, 1601

Human figure alphabet. Italy, 17th cn.

Human figure alphabet. Italy, 17th cn.

France, 17th cn.

France, 17th cn.

Dreamer's alphabet by Giuseppe Mitelli, Bologne, 1683

Dreamer's alphabet by Giuseppe Mitelli, Bologne, 1683

France, 17th cn.

Portugal, 17th cn.

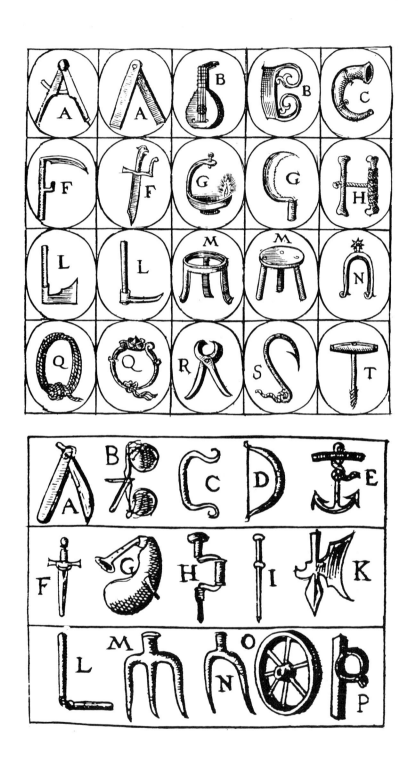

France, 17th cn.

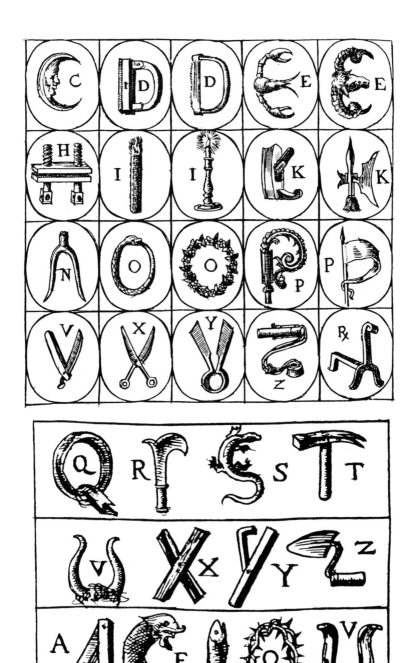

France, 17th cn.

Rococo alphabet, 18th cn.

Rococo alphabet, 18th cn.

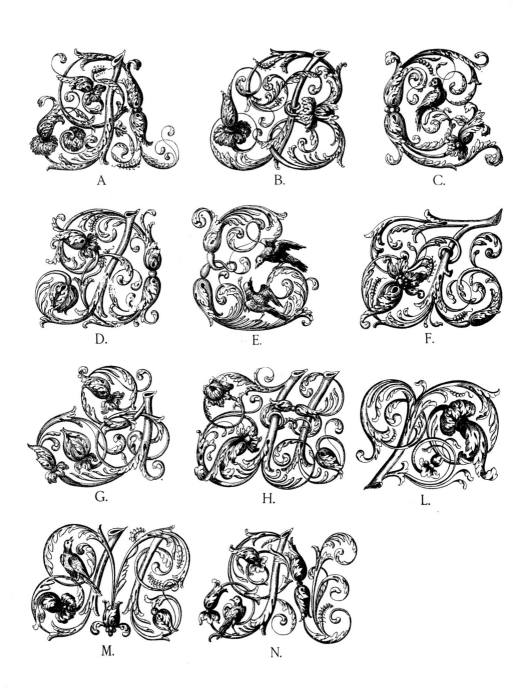

A   B.   C.

D.   E.   F.

G.   H.   L.

M.   N.

Alphabet in Rococo style by Manuel de Andrade, Lisbon, 1719

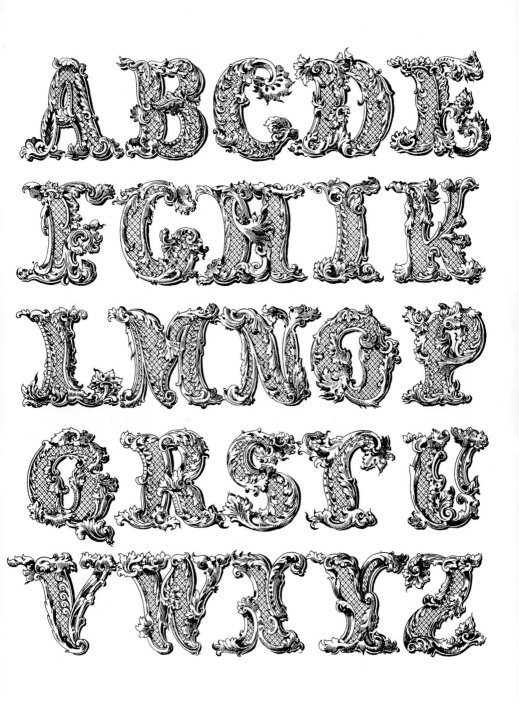

Rococo alphabet, 18th cn.

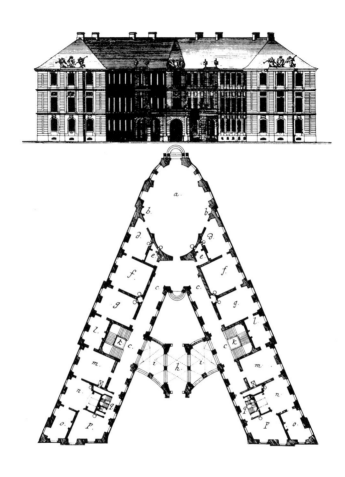

Johann David Steingruber, Architectural alphabet, 1773. Each letter corresponds to the plan of a building.

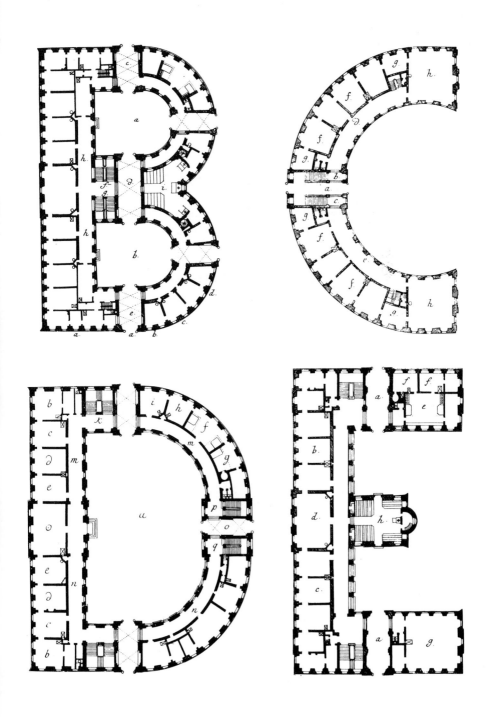

Johann David Steingruber, Architectural alphabet, 1773. Each letter corresponds to the plan
of a building.

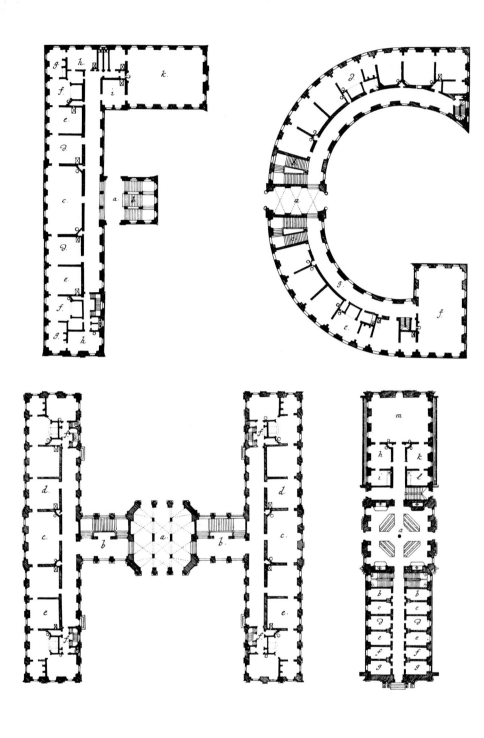

Johann David Steingruber, Architectural alphabet, 1773. Each letter corresponds to the plan of a building.

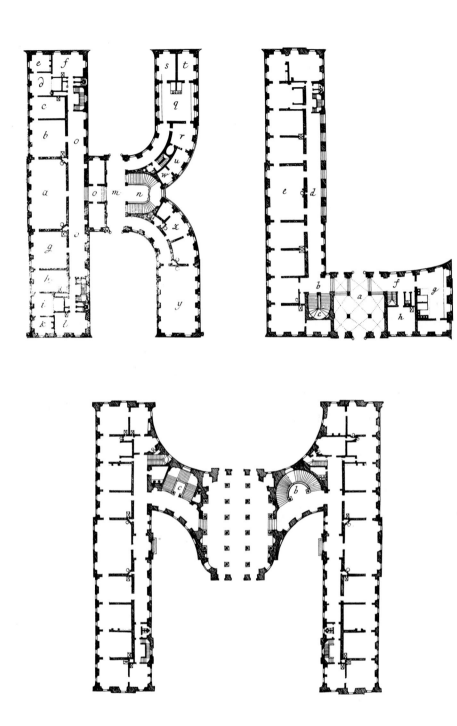

Johann David Steingruber, Architectural alphabet, 1773. Each letter corresponds to the plan of a building.

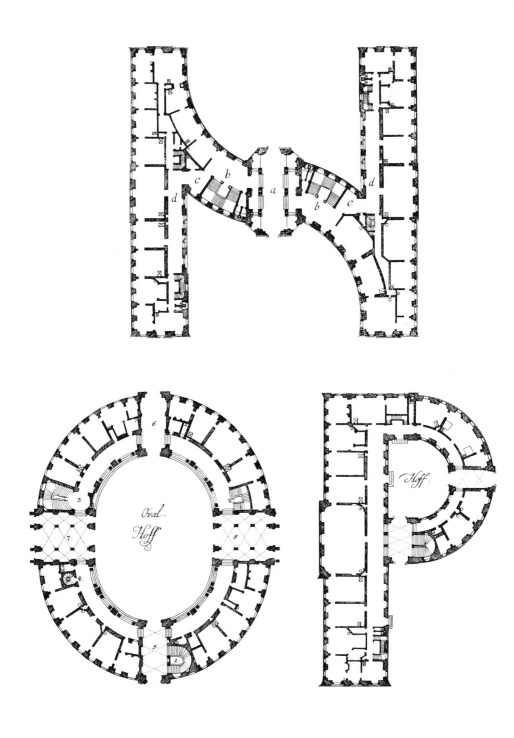

Johann David Steingruber, Architectural alphabet, 1773. Each letter corresponds to the plan of a building.

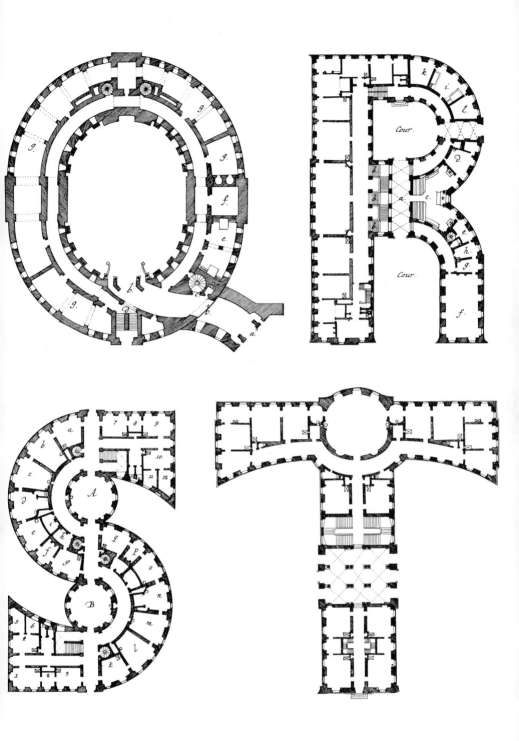

Johann David Steingruber, Architectural alphabet, 1773. Each letter corresponds to the plan of a building.

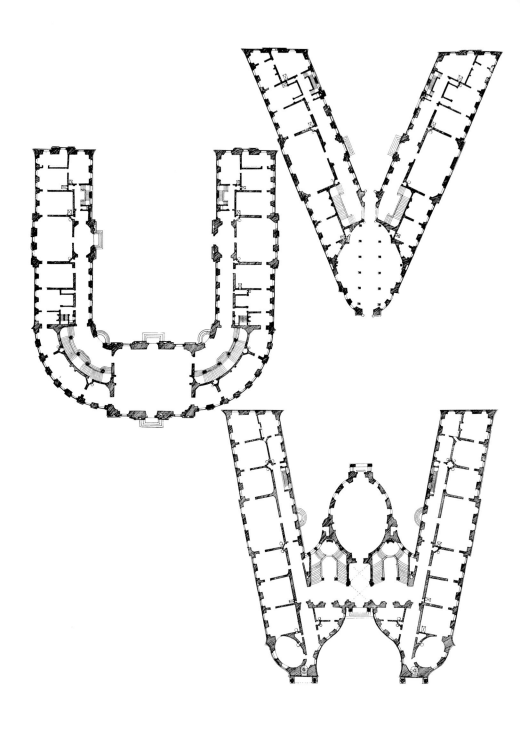

Johann David Steingruber, Architectural alphabet, 1773. Each letter corresponds to the plan of a building.

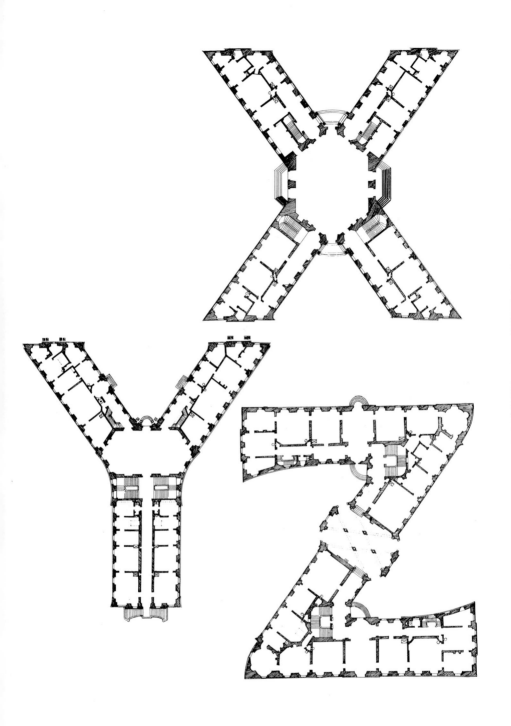

Johann David Steingruber, Architectural alphabet, 1773. Each letter corresponds to the plan of a building.

From a manuscript from the monastery of St. Geneviève, Paris, 18th cn.

From a manuscript from the monastery of St. Geneviève, Paris, 18th cn.

Woodcut initials by Jean Michel Papillon, Paris, 1760

Woodcut initials by Jean Michel Papillon, Paris, 1760

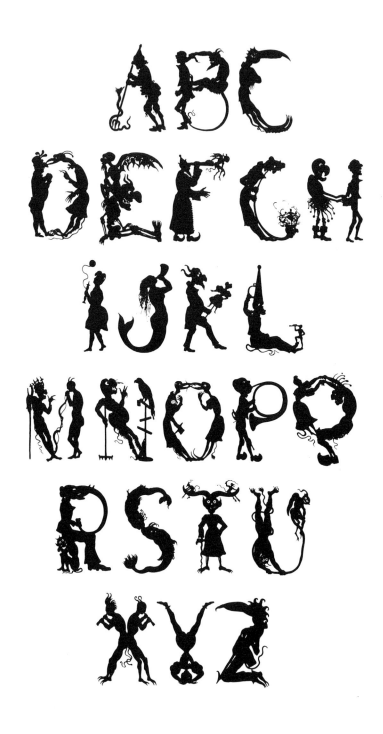

Alphabet diabolique, end of the 18th cn.

Human figure alphabet, beginning of the 19th cn.

Animal alphabet, Great Britain (?), beginning of the 19th cn.

Animal alphabet, Great Britain (?), beginning of the 19th cn.

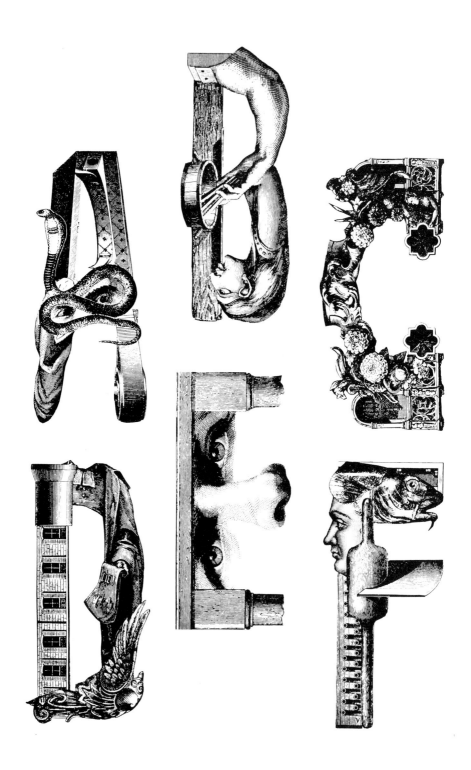

Fanciful alphabet, America, beginning of the 19th cn.

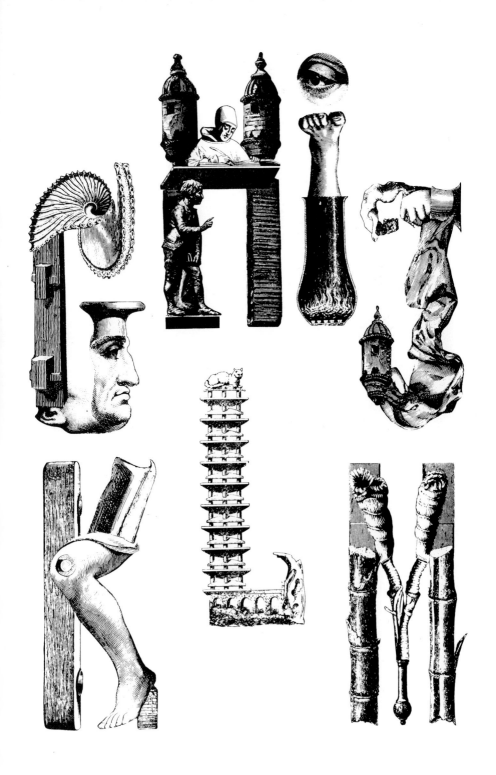

Fanciful alphabet, America, beginning of the 19th cn.

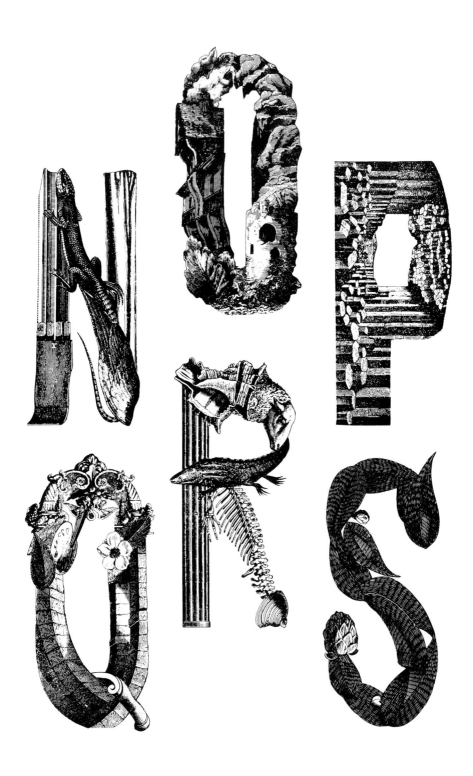

Fanciful alphabet, America, beginning of the 19th cn.

Fanciful alphabet, America, beginning of the 19th cn.

Animal alphabet, France, 19th cn.

Tree alphabet, France, 19th cn.

From a Venetian Manuscript of the 15th cn., 19th cn.

After an alphabet by Vespasiano, Venice, 17th cn. 19th cn.

After an alphabet by Vespasiano, Venice, 17th cn. 19th cn.

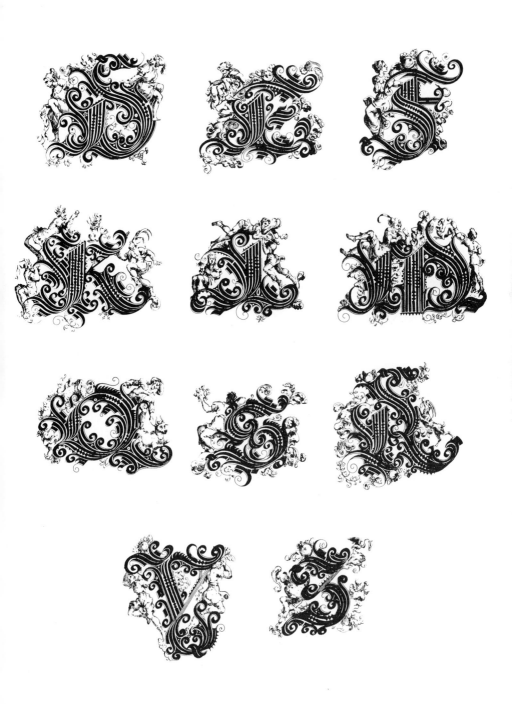

After an alphabet by Vespasiano, Venice, 17th cn. 19th cn.

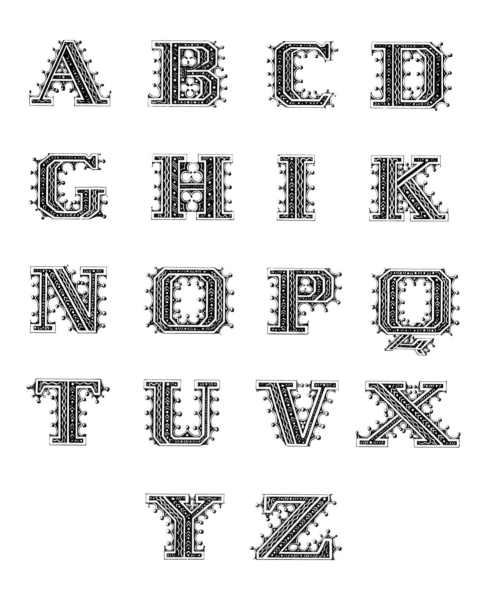

Gothic-style letters by J. Midolle, Strasbourg, 1834/35

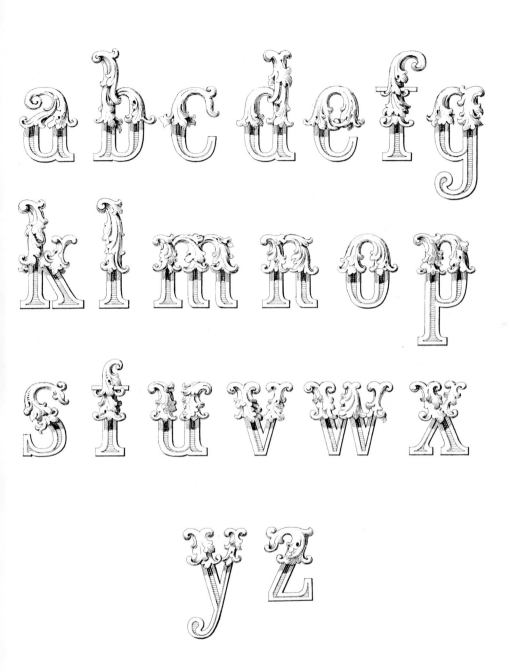

Decorative lettering by Karl Klimsch, middle of the 19th cn.

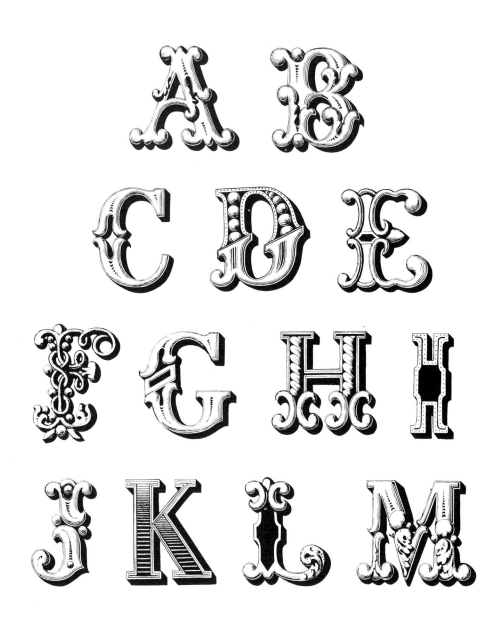

Decorative initials derived from baroque style, 19th cn.

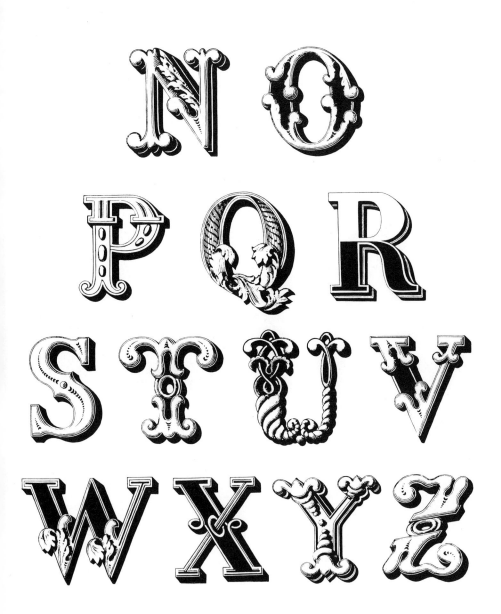

Decorative initials derived from baroque style, 19th cn.

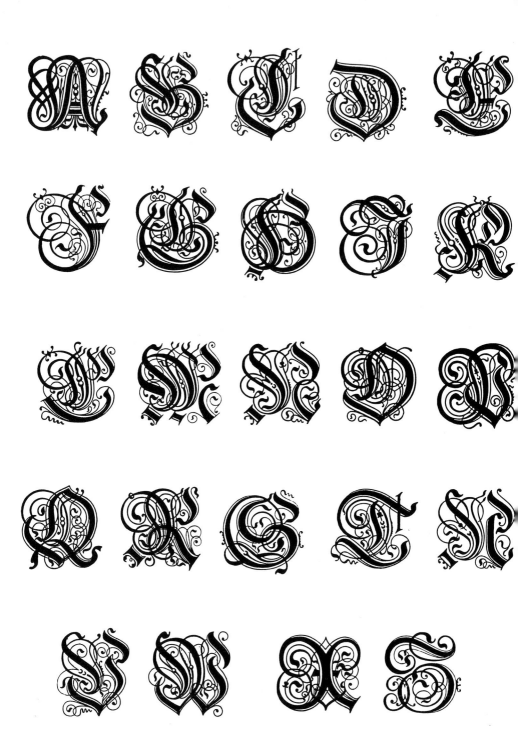

Schwabacher initials. Munich, ca. 1880

After 18th cn. alphabets. Germany, 19th cn.

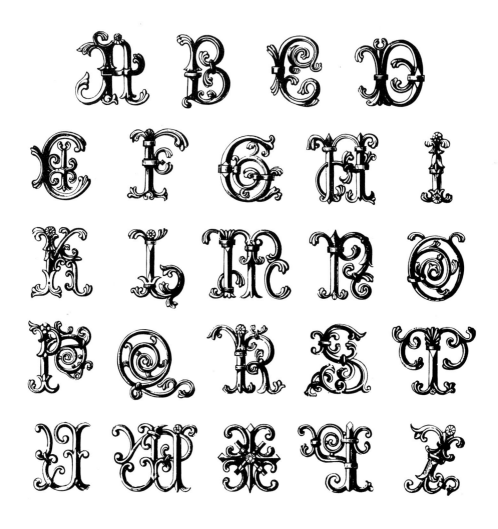

England, 19th cn.

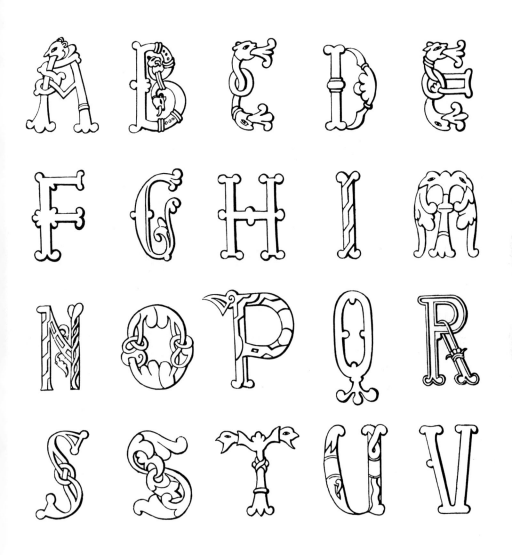

After Celtic ornamental alphabets. England, 19th cn.

America, 19th cn.

America, 19th cn.

Fraktur initials in gothic style, 19th cn.

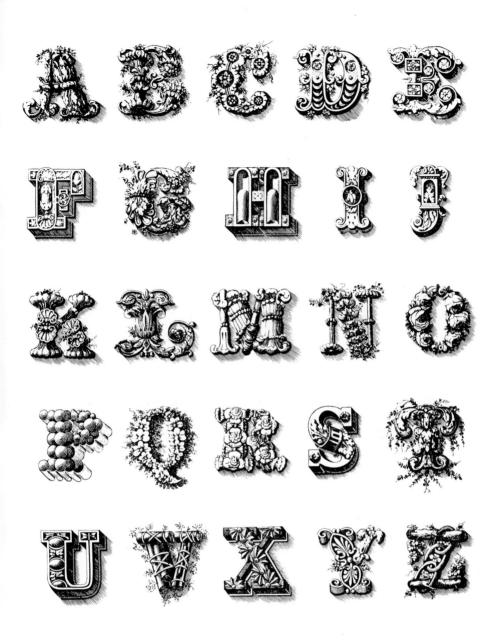

Italy, designed by D. Biagio and Constantine Santerini, 19th cn.

After Gothic models, England, 19th cn.

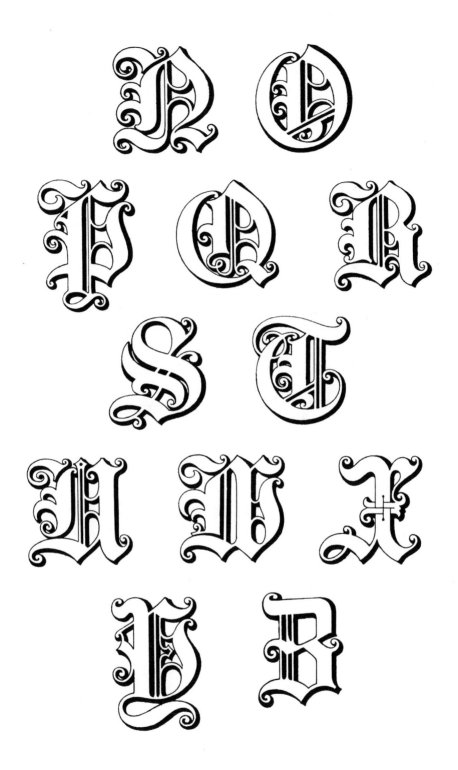

After Gothic models, England, 19th cn.

Decorative lettering by J. Midolle, 19th cn.

Alphabet based on Greek ornamentation by J. Midolle, 19th cn.

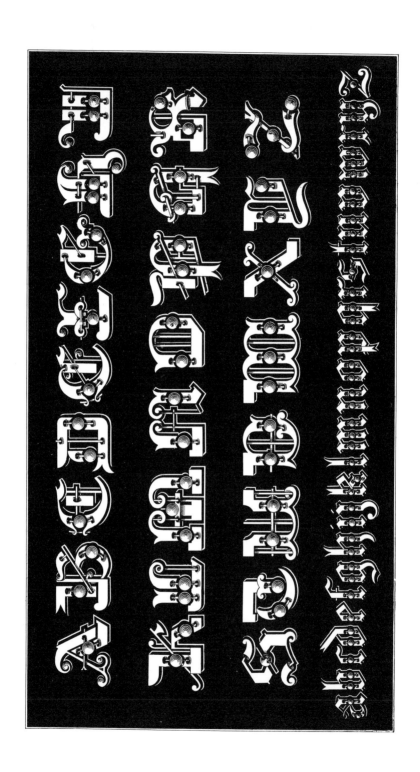

After Renaissance original. Silvestre, 19th cn.

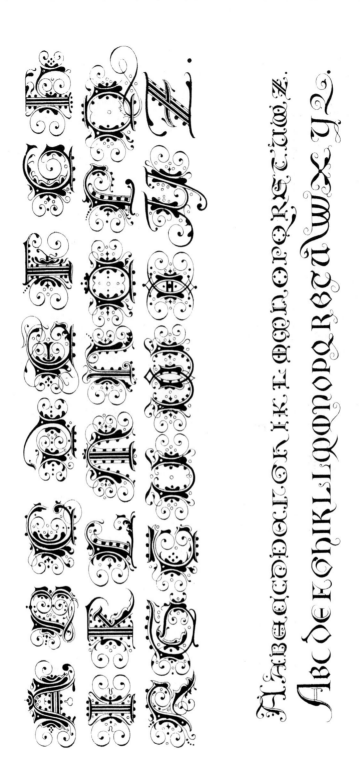

After a manuscript in the Bayerische Staatsbibliothek, Munich. Silvestre, 19th cn.

Decorative letters after Gothic originals, 19th cn.

Decorative letters after Gothic originals, 19th cn.

Copied after a manuscript in the library of Bologna. Silvestre, 19th cn.

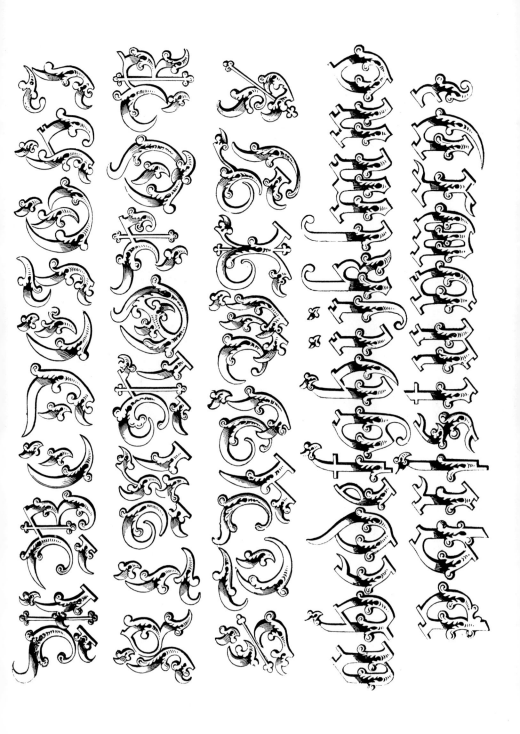

Revival of German baroque letters with Victorian styling, 1859

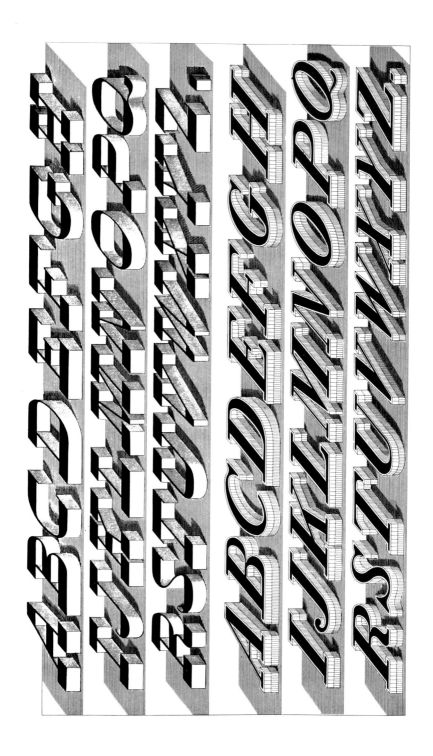

Three-dimensional letters. Silvestre, 19th cn.

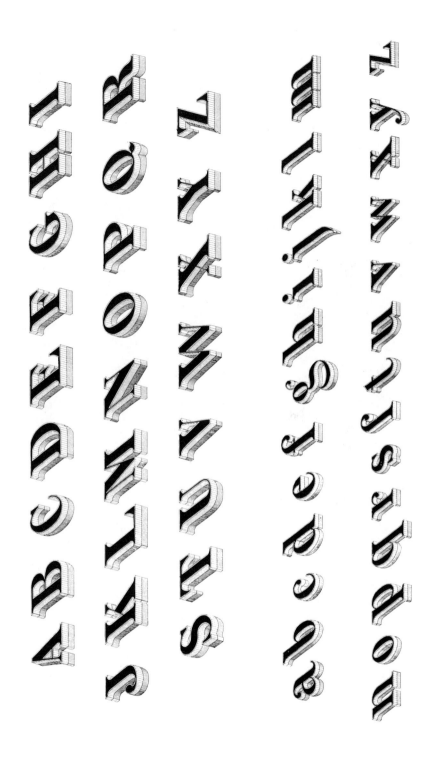

Three-dimensional letters. Silvestre, 19th cn.

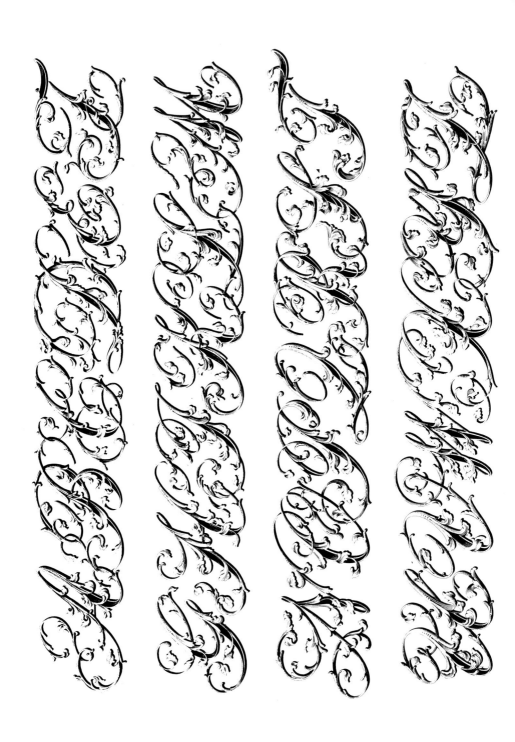

Initialen with arabesque design. Silvestre, 19th cn.

Foliated script capitals. Silvestre, 19th cn. Three-dimensional alphabet, 19th cn.

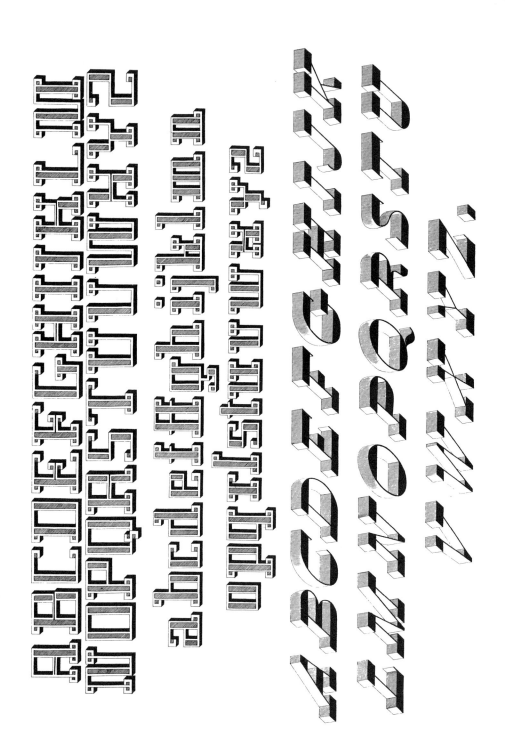

Imaginative alphabets. Silvestre, 19th cn.

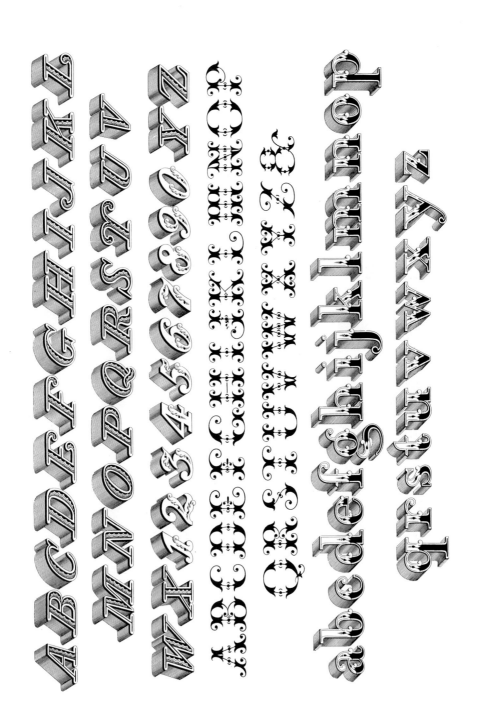

Alphabets by R. Stirling, 19th cn.

Alphabets by R. Stirling, 19th cn.

Decorative lettering by Silvestre, 19th cn.

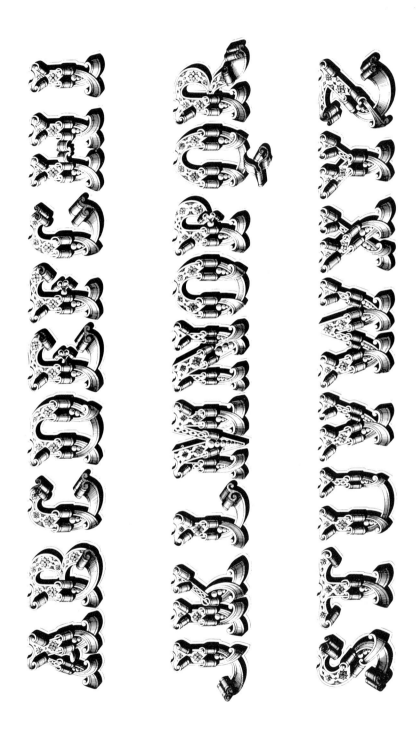

Alphabet by R. Stirling, 19th cn.

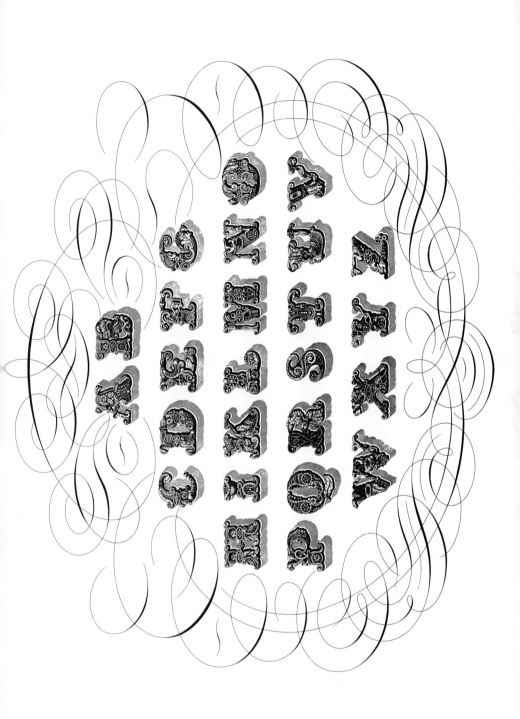

Composite capitals by J. Midolle, 19th cn.

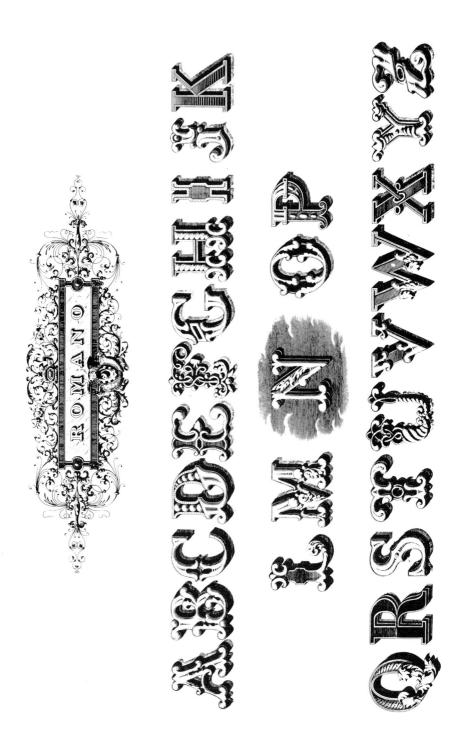

Alphabets by R. Stirling, 19th cn.

Alphabets by R. Stirling, 19th cn.

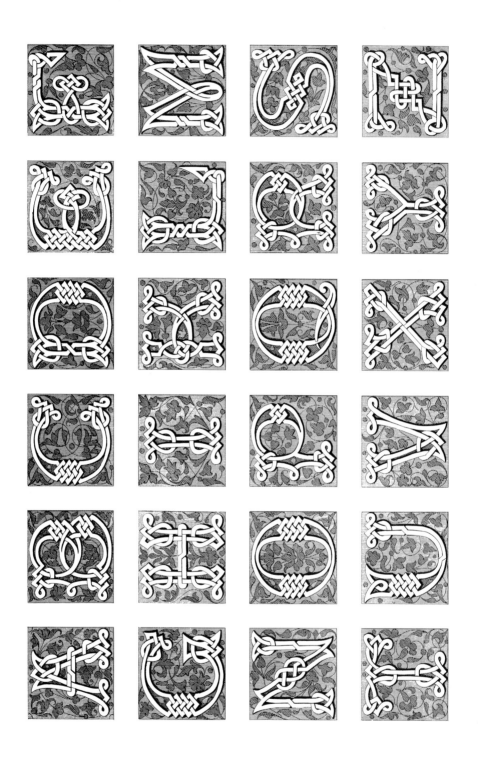

Imitation of Saxon letters by Silvestre, 19th cn.

Alphabet by R. Stirling, 19th cn.

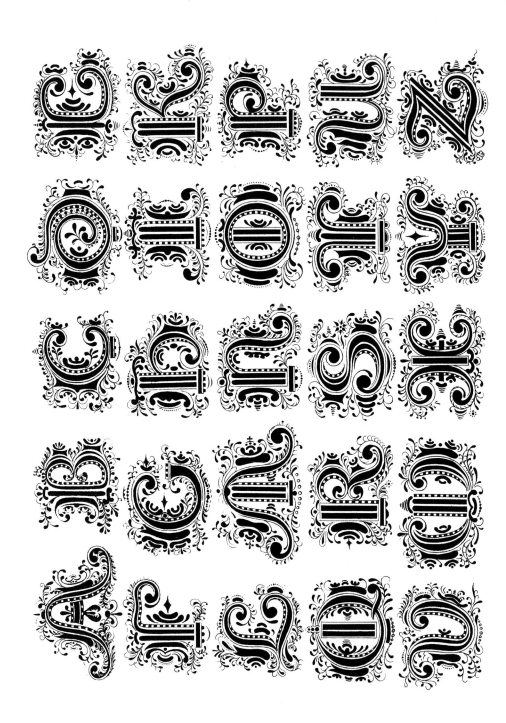

From a manuscript in Vienna, 18th cn. Silvestre, 19th cn.

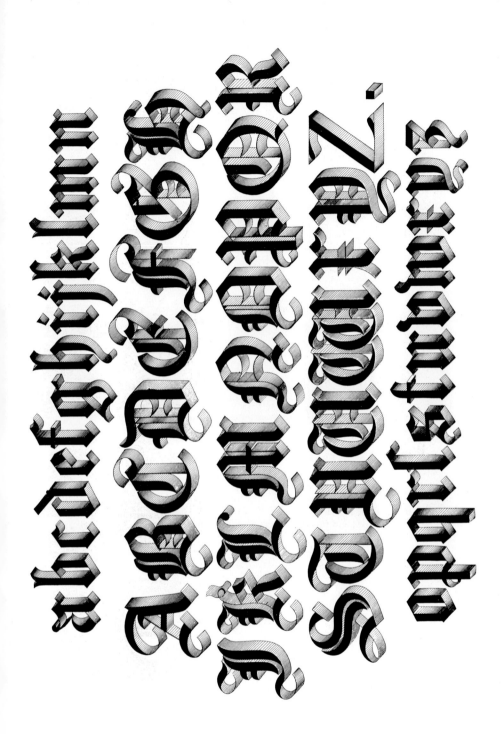

Three-dimensional Gothic alphabet by Silvestre, 19th cn.

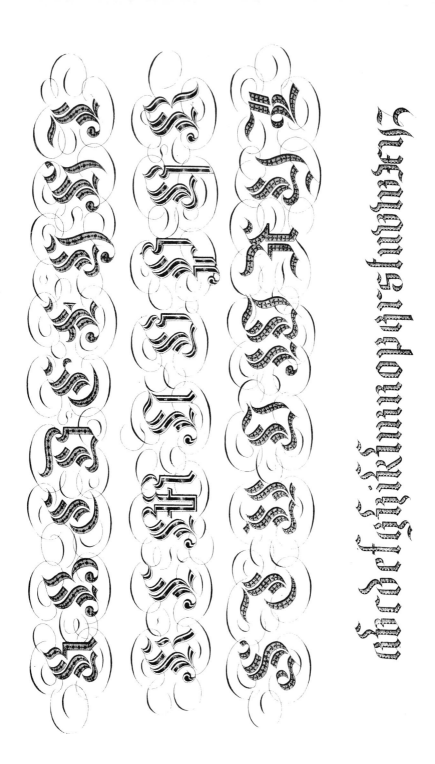

After Gothic models by J. Midolle, 19th cn.

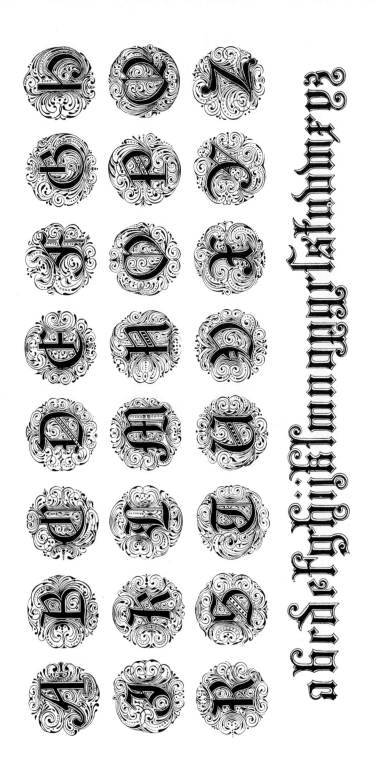

From a manuscript in Vienna. Silvestre, 19th cn.

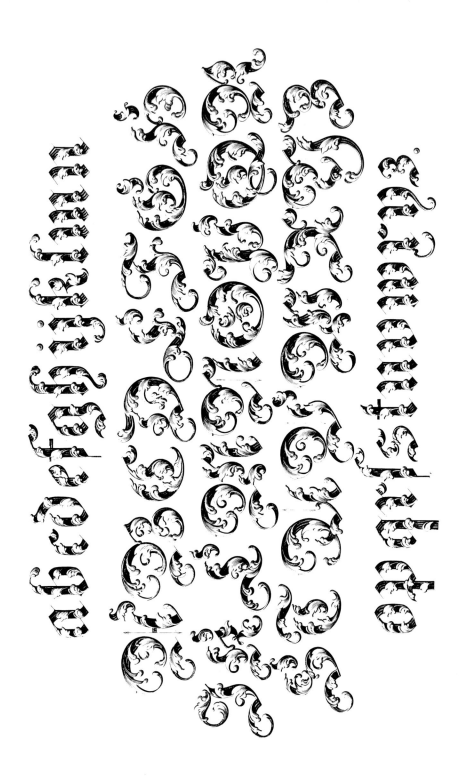

Foliated Gothic alphabet. Silvestre, 19th cn.

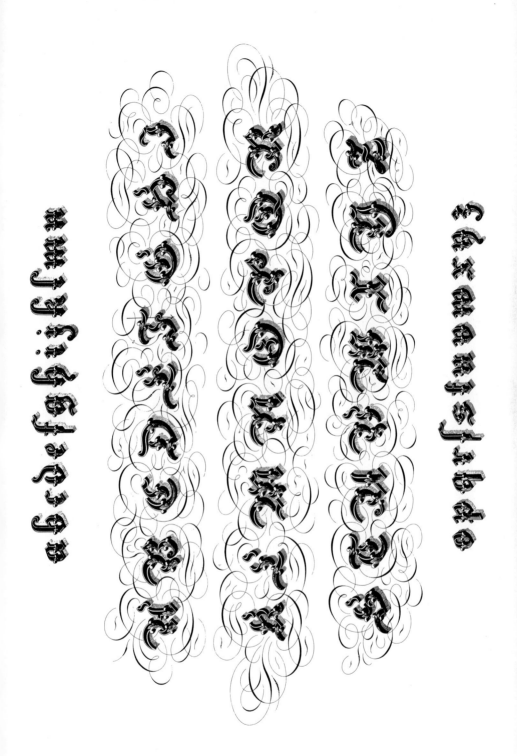

Alphabet by Silvestre, 19th cn.

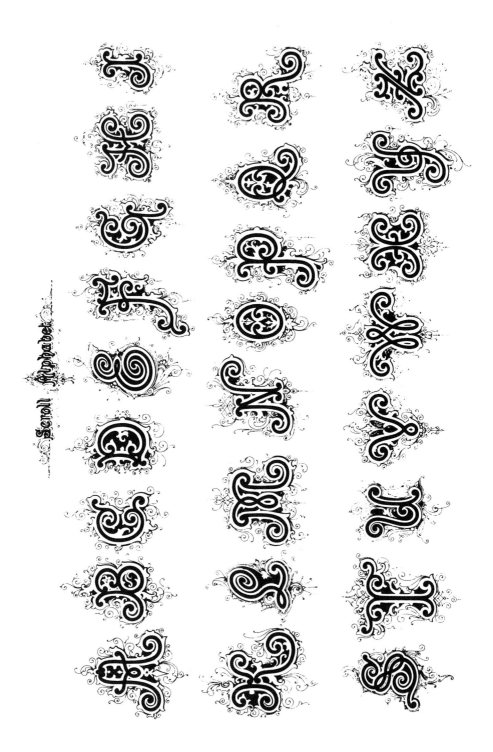

Alphabet with tendril decorations, 19 th cn.

Rustic Alphabet

Alphabet with tendril decorations, 19 th cn.

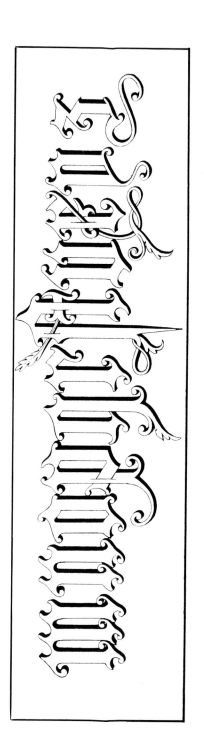

Gothic lapidary alphabet. Silvestre, 19th cn.

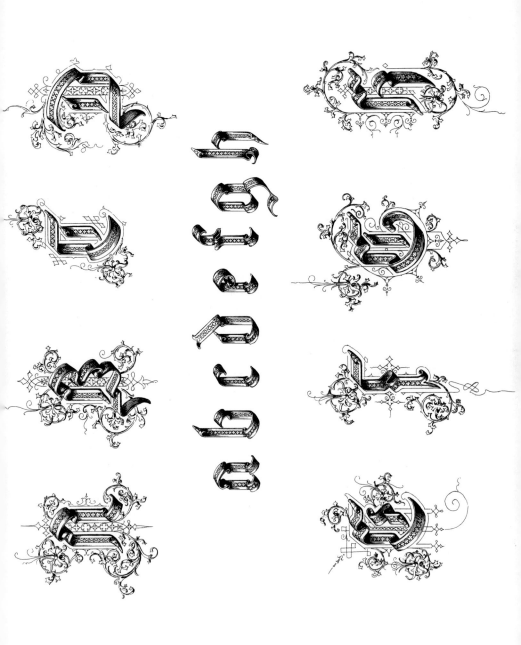

Decorative lettering by Karl Klimsch, 19th cn.

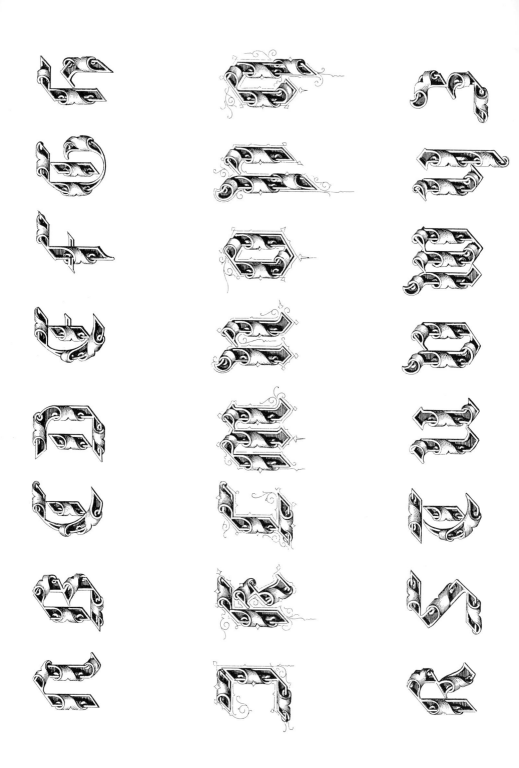

Decorative lettering by Karl Klimsch, 19th cn.

Decorative lettering by Karl Klimsch, 19th cn.

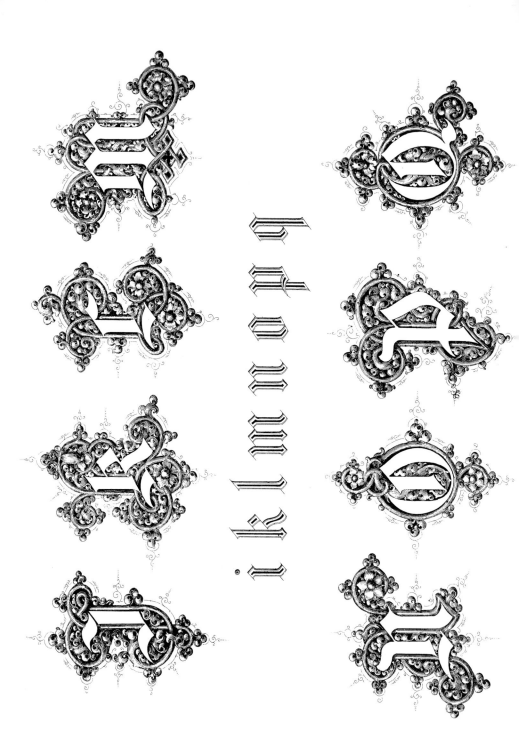

Decorative lettering by Karl Klimsch, 19th cn.

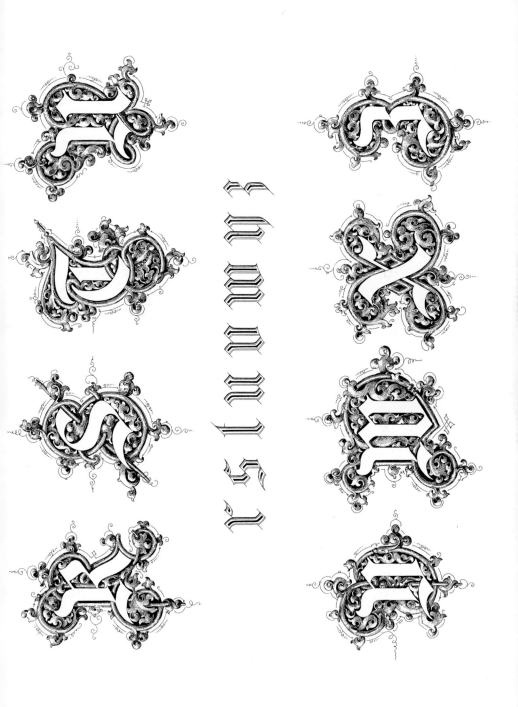

Decorative lettering by Karl Klimsch, 19th cn.

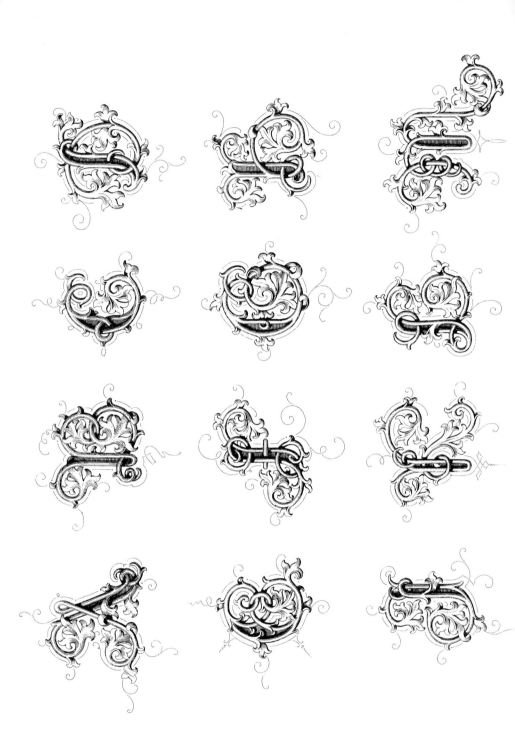

Decorative lettering by Karl Klimsch, 19th cn.

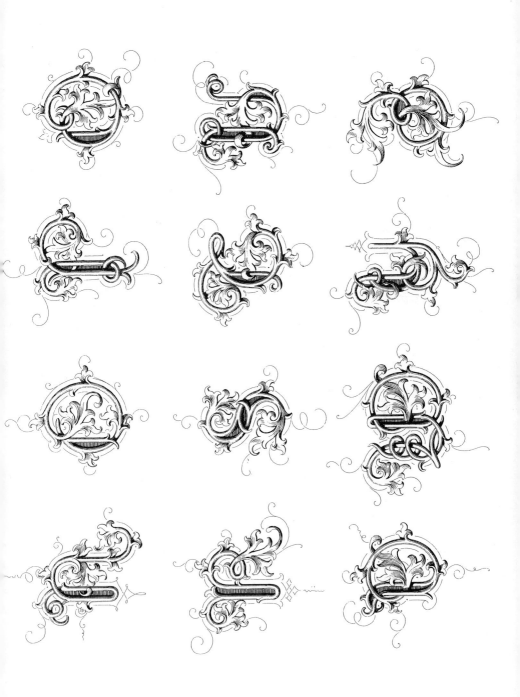

Decorative lettering by Karl Klimsch, 19th cn.

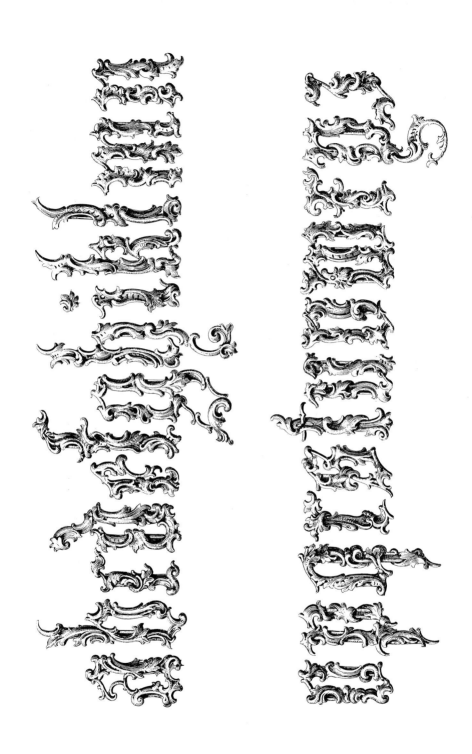

Decorative lettering by Karl Klimsch, 19th cn.

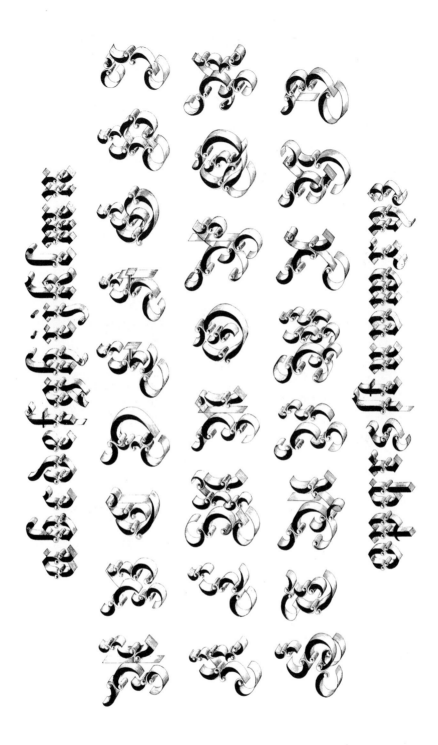

Three-dimensional initials after Gothic models. Silvestre, 19th cn.

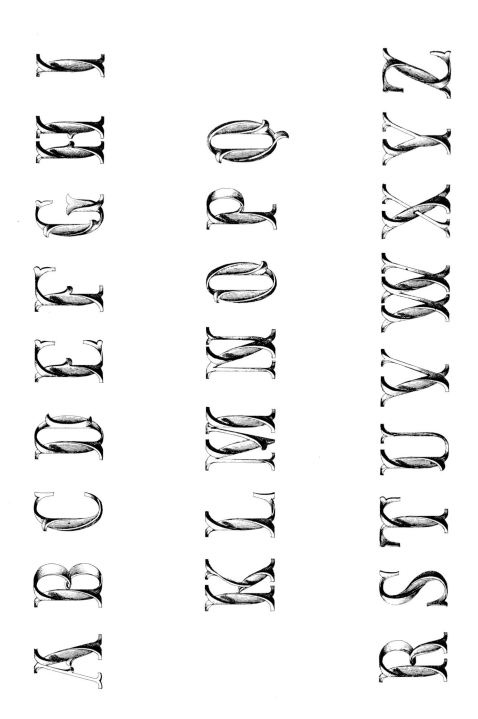

Decorative lettering by Karl Klimsch, 19th cn.

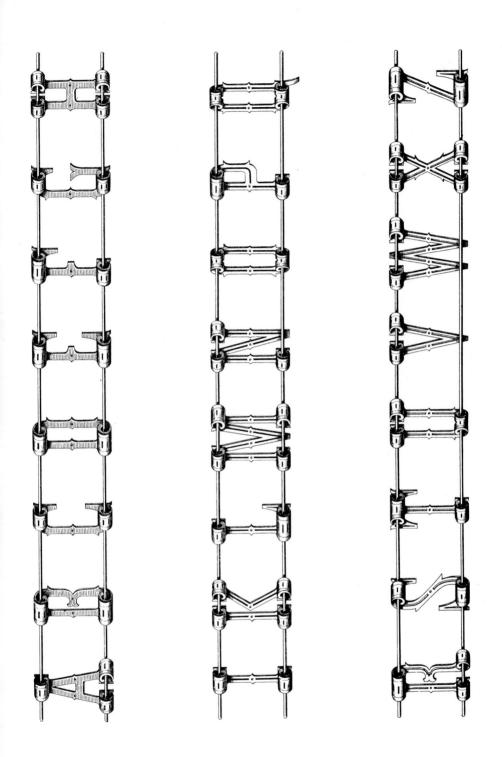

Decorative lettering by Karl Klimsch, 19th cn.

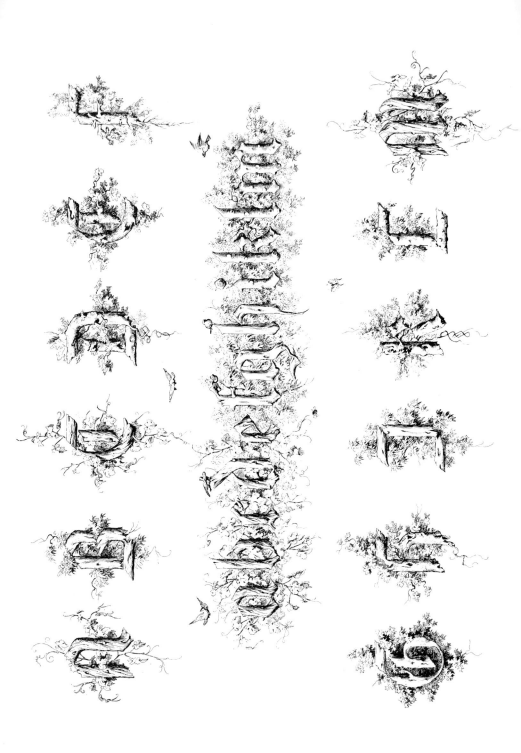

Decorative lettering by Karl Klimsch, 19th cn.

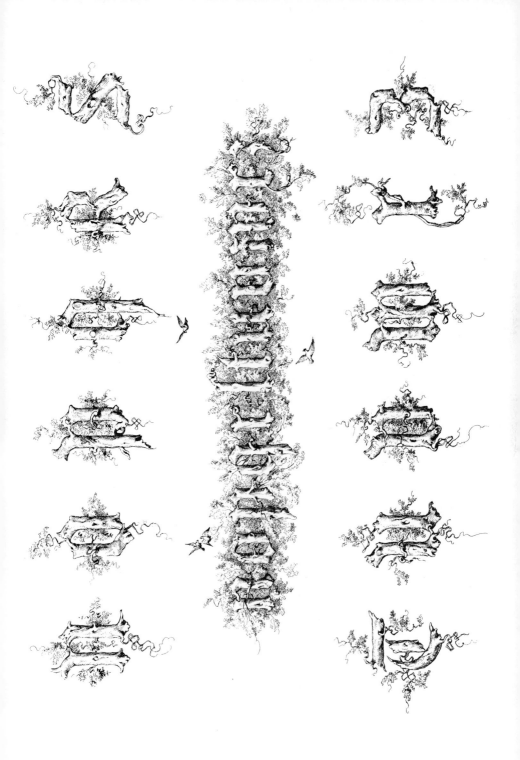

Decorative lettering by Karl Klimsch, 19th cn.

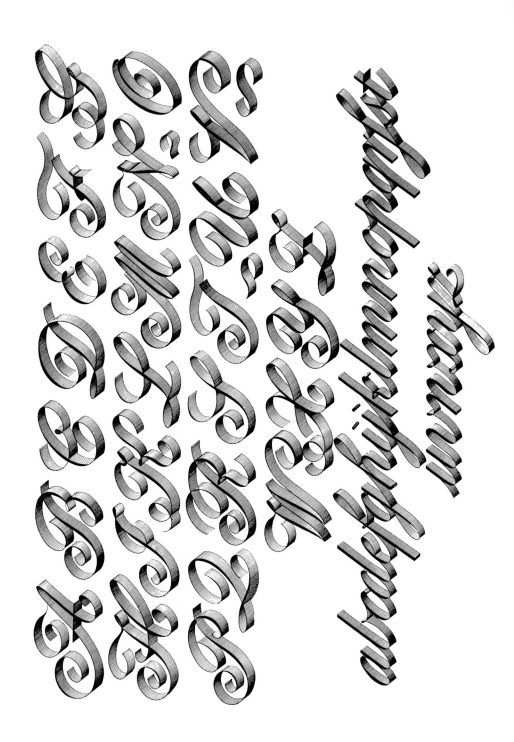

Ribbon script letters. Silvestre, 19th cn.

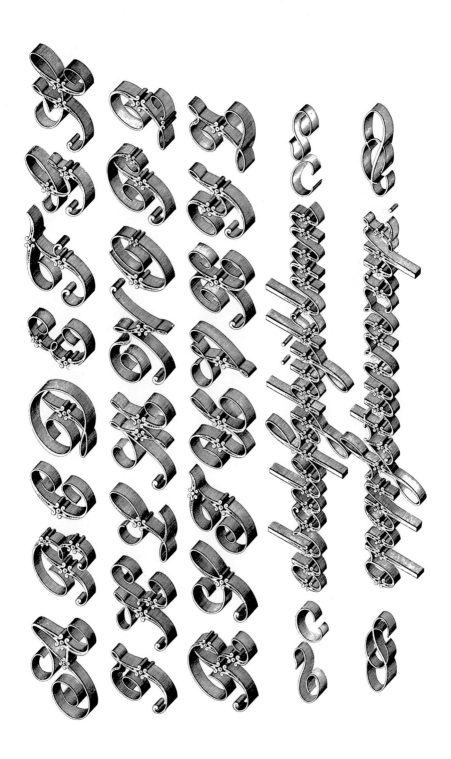

Ribbon script letters. Silvestre, 19th cn.

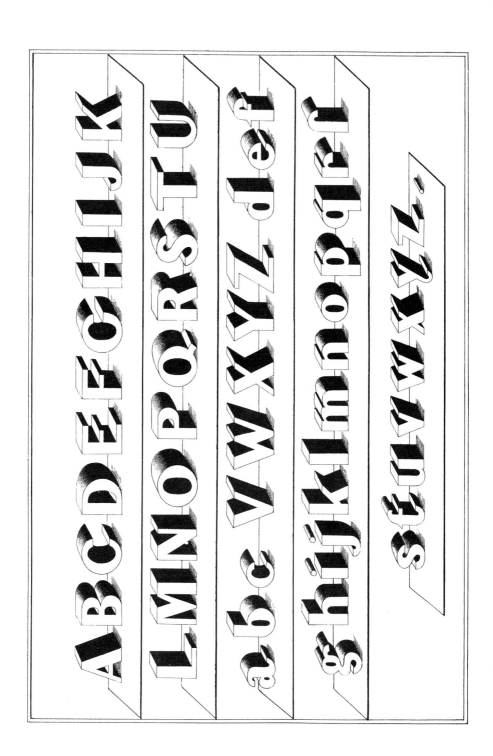

Woodcut alphabet, by Silvestre, 19th cn.

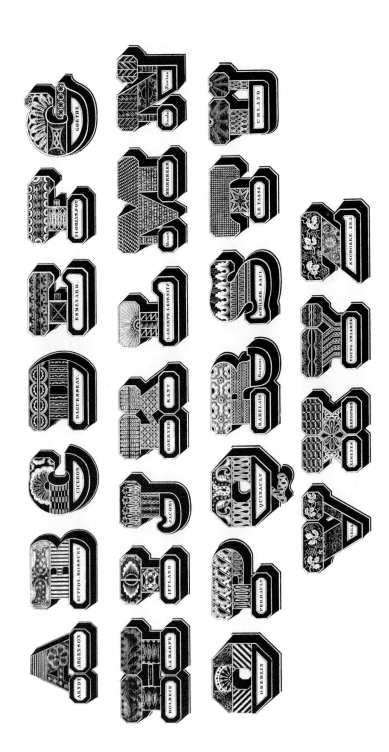

Composite capitals by J. Midolle, 19th cn.

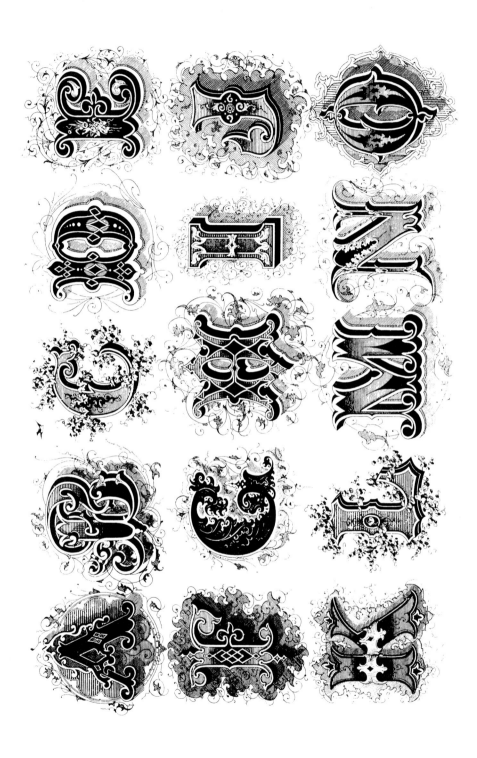

Initials by Daniel T. Ames, New York, 1879

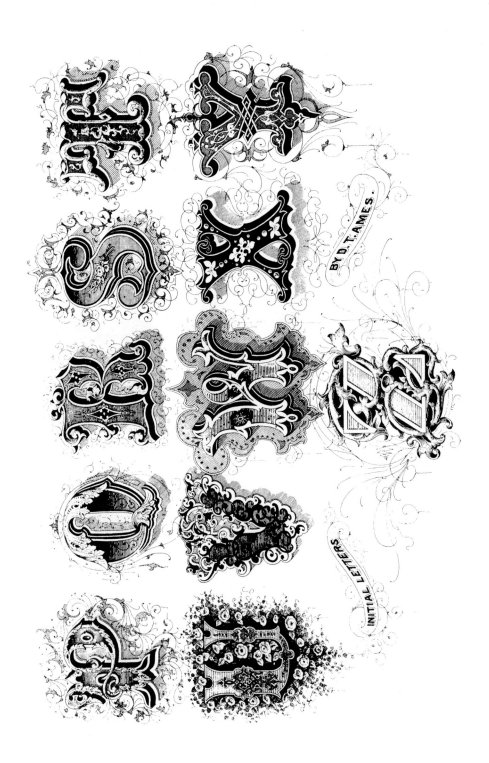

Initials by Daniel T. Ames, New York, 1879

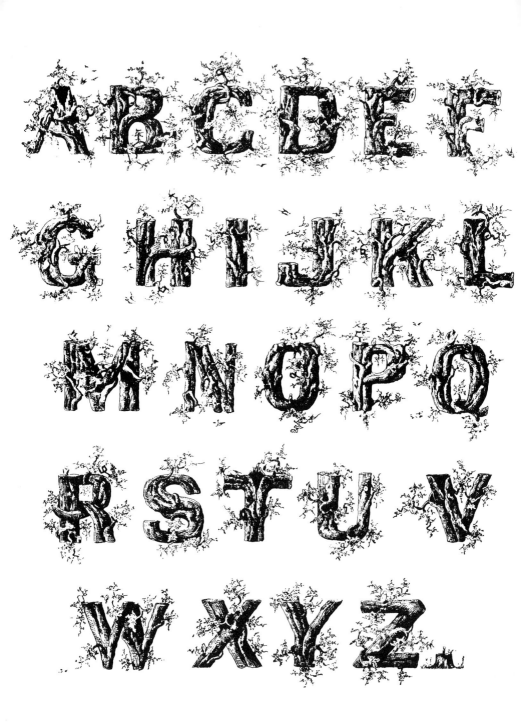

Tree alphabet, 19th cn.

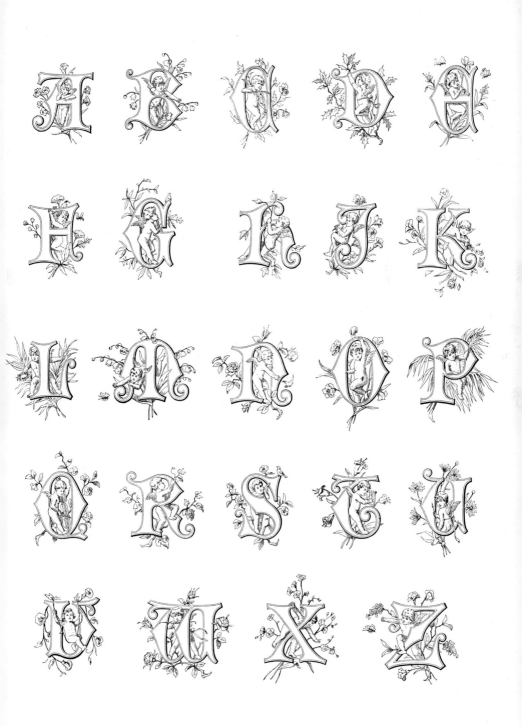

Children alphabet, 19th cn.

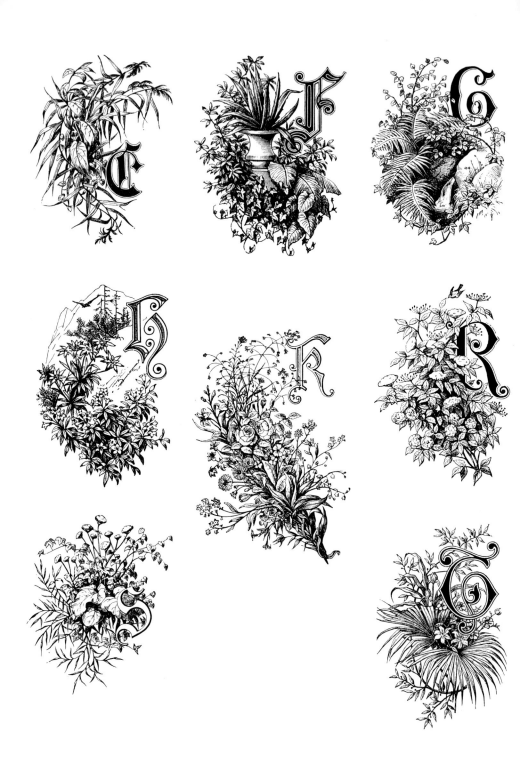

Plant initials, America, ca. 1880

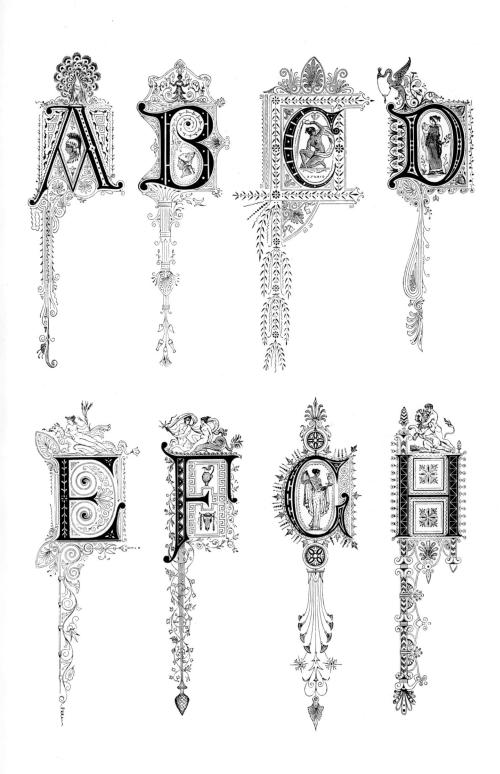

Composite capitals, 1889

Decorative lettering by Karl Klimsch, 19th cn.

Decorative lettering by Karl Klimsch, 19th cn.

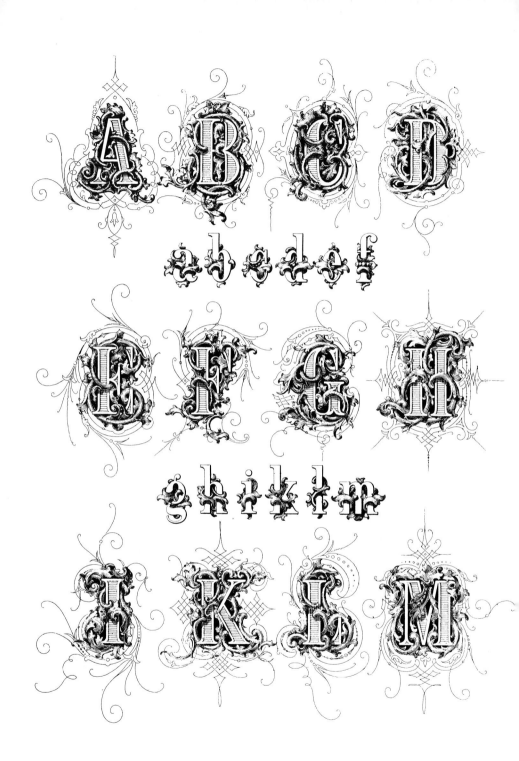

Decorative lettering by Karl Klimsch, 19th cn.

Decorative lettering by Karl Klimsch, 19th cn.

Fanciful alphabet. America, end of the 19th cn.

Fanciful alphabet. America, end of the 19th cn.

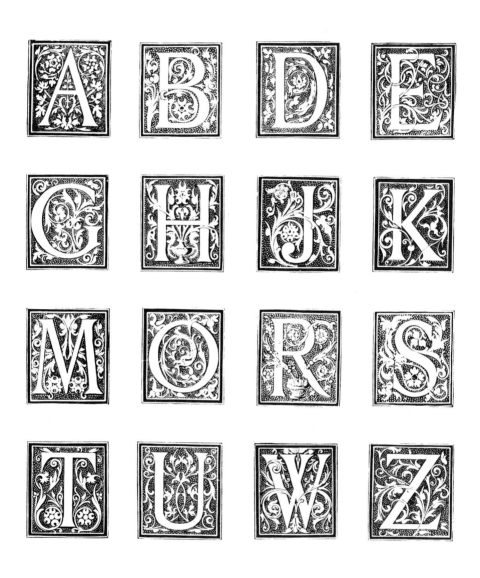

After Florentine alphabets. Germany, 20th cn.

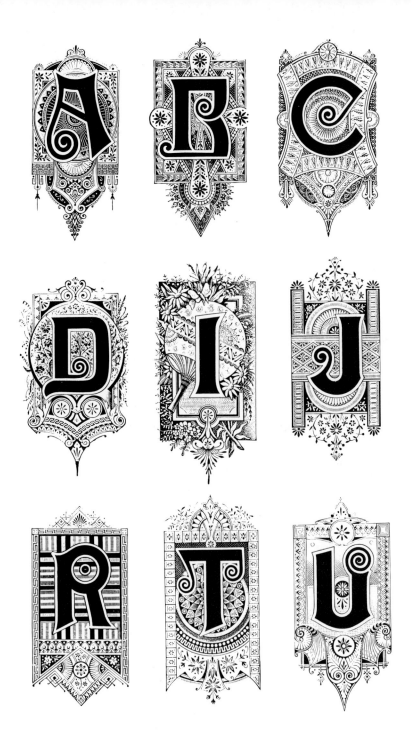

Fanciful alphabet, America, 20th cn.

Copies of Plantin initials (16th cn.) by Thomas Cleland, 20th cn.

Copies of Plantin initials (16th cn.) by Thomas Cleland, 20th cn.

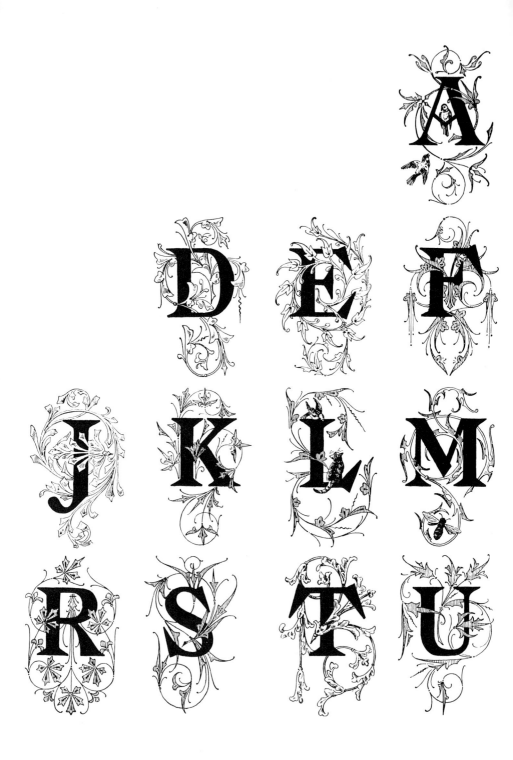

Initials with tendril decorations. America, 20th cn.

Initials with tendril decorations. America, 20th cn.

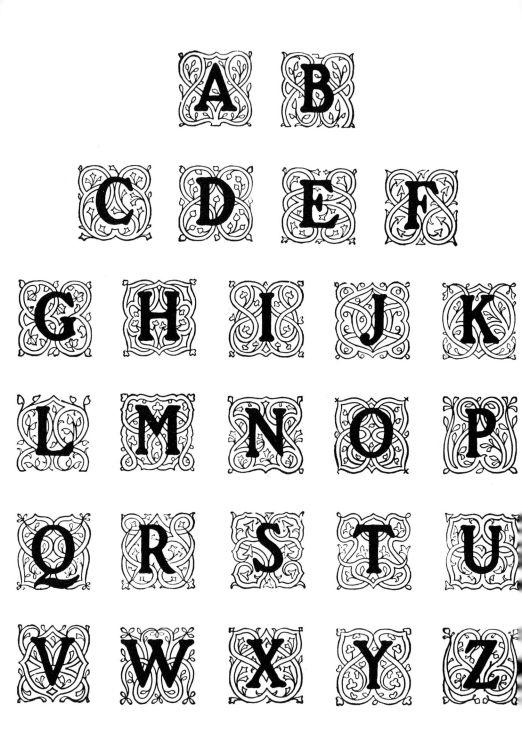

Initials with tendril decorations. America, 20th cn.

Initials with wickerwork. Frankreich, 20th cn.

Decorative letters from "Morte d'Arthur" by Aubrey Beardsley, 1893

Decorative letters by Otto Eckmann, ca. 1900

Roman initials from the magazine "Pan" and book ornaments by F. H. Ehmcke, 1904

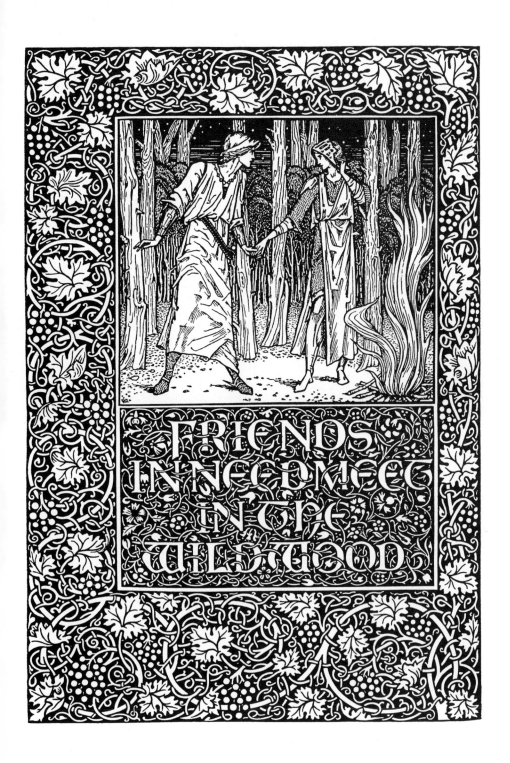

FRIENDS IN NEED MEET IN THE WILD WOOD

Letters derived from Gothic models by Charles W. Morris, ca. 1895

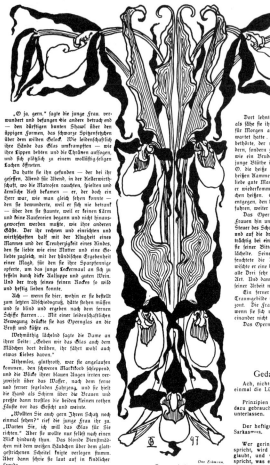

„O ja, gern." sagte die junge Frau, verwundert und befangen die andere betrachtend — den dürftigen bunten Shawl über den üppigen Formen, das schwarze Spitzentüchchen über dem wilden Gelock. Wie leidenschaftlich ihre Hände das Glas umkrampften — wie ihre Lippen bebten und die Thränen aufsogen, und sich plötzlich zu einem wollüstig-seligen Lachen öffneten.

Da hatte sie ihn gefunden — der bei ihr gesessen, Abend für Abend, in der Kellerwirthschaft, wo die Matrosen rauchten, spielten und ärmliche Kost bekamen — er, der doch ein Herr war, wie man gleich sehen konnte — den sie bewunderte, weil er sich nie betrank — über den sie staunte, weil er keinen Lärm und keine Raufereien begann und nicht hinausgeworfen werden mußte, wie die anderen Gäste. Der ihr rechnen und einrichten und wirthschaften half mit der Klugheit eines Mannes und der Treuherzigkeit eines Kindes, den sie liebte zugleich, mit der hündischen Ergebenheit einer Magd, für den sie ihre Sparpfennige opferte, um das junge Leckermaul an sich zu fesseln durch dicke Aalsuppe und guten Wein. Und der trotz seines feinen Rockes so wild und heftig lieben konnte.

Ach — wenn sie hier, wohin er sie bestellt zum letzten Abschiedsgruß, hätte sehen müssen und so blind und ergeben nach dem fernen Schiffe starren ... Mit einer leidenschaftlichen Bewegung drückte sie das Opernglas an die Brust und küßte es.

Wehmüthig lächelnd sagte die Dame an ihrer Seite: „Geben wir das Glas auch dem Mädchen dort drüben, ihr fährt wohl auch etwas Liebes davon."

Athemlos, gluthroth, war sie angelaufen gekommen, den schweren Marktkorb schleppend, und die Blicke ihrer blauen Augen irrten verzweifelt über das Wasser, nach dem ferne und ferner segelnden Fahrzeug, und sie hielt die Hand als Schirm über die Brauen und preßte dann trostlos die beiden kleinen rothen Fäuste vor das Gesicht und weinte.

„Wollten Sie auch gern Ihren Schatz noch einmal sehen?" rief die junge Frau ihr zu. „Warten Sie, ich will das Glas für Sie richten." Aber sie wollte nur selbst nach einen Blick hindurch thun. Das blonde Dienstmädchen mit dem weißen Häubchen über dem glattgestrichenen Scheitel knixte verlegen stumm. Aber dann schrie sie laut auf in kindlicher Freude.

Dort lehnte er am Steuerbord — gleich als sähe sie ihn dicht vor sich, wie er Morgen für Morgen an der Straßenecke auf sie gewartet hatte ... Dessen frohe Munterkeit sie bethörte, der nicht grob forderte wie die andern, sondern zart und gütig mit ihr umging, wie ein Bruder, bis sie ihm willenlos die junge Blüthe ihres Leibes zum Opfer brachte. O, die heiße glückliche Nacht in der kleinen heißen Kammer unter dem Dache ... O, der liebe gute Mann ... In einem Jahr, wenn er wiederkommen würde, sollte sie sein Weibchen heißen. Gläubig lächelte sie der Ferne entgegen, den Hoffnungen zu, die dort hinausfuhren, den Hoffnungen zu, die dort hinausfuhren — immer weiter ....

Das Opernglas wanderte zwischen den Frauen hin und wieder. Und der Mann am Steuer des Schooners blickte nach dem Strande und auf die drei Gestalten, die dort so einträchtig bei einander standen. Wie gehorsam sie seiner Bitte gefolgt waren .... Und er lächelte. Seine treuherzigen braunen Augen feuchtete eine Thräne fort. Er hatte sie doch alle Drei sehr gern gehabt — jede in ihrer Art. Und dann wandte er sich um und ging seiner Arbeit nach.

Ein ferner weißer Schemen, ein zartes Traumgebilde verschwand das Schiff am Horizont. Die Frauen tauschten einen Gruß und wenn sie sich wieder begegneten, kannten sie einander nicht mehr.

Das Opernglas hatte nichts verrathen.

Gedanken von Multatuli

Ach, nichts ist vollkommen ... nicht einmal die Lügen.

Prinzipien sind Dinge, welche man dazu gebraucht, etwas Unangenehmes zu unterlassen.

Der heftigste Schmerz äussert sich in Sarkasmus.

Wer geringschätzig über sich selbst spricht, wird ärgerlich, wenn man ihm glaubt, und wüthend, wenn man nachspricht, was er gesagt hat.

(Aus dem Holländischen übersetzt von E. O.)

Frauenschuh — *Otto Eckmann*

Integrated row ornament by Otto Eckmann, 1897
Initials by Peter Behrens, 1908

Warum
der kleine Fritzi durchaus nicht in den Kindergarten wollte
(Eine wohlweise Geschichte)

Als der kleine Fritzi hörte, daß er in den Kindergarten solle, da zeigte sich, daß die Eltern ihn von seiner allerunliebenswürdigsten Seite noch nicht einmal kennen gelernt hatten. Er schrie so gewaltig, daß nach fünf Minuten die Züge 2, 5 und 6 der Feuerwehr zur Stelle waren, und trommelte mit seinen Füßen so heftig und gleichmäßig gegen Thür, Kommode, Eckschrank und Bauch des Vaters, daß die Zeitungen am nächsten Tage von einer „erdbebenartigen Erscheinung" berichteten.

Die kindliche Psyche gibt oft dem ältesten und weisesten Manne unlösbare Räthsel auf, und so beschloß denn auch der Vater des kleinen Fritzi, vorderhand von jeglichem Zwange abzusehen und sich abwartend zu verhalten.

„Es gibt in der kindlichen Seele Sympathien und Antipathien, ja, man kann wohl sagen: Idiosynkrasien, die sich selbst unserer Einsicht verschließen," sagte der Vater, ein oft examinirter Mann, zu seiner Gattin.

Diese, als sie alle die griechischen Wörter hörte, wollte sorgenvoll nach einem Arzte schicken, aber der Haushaltungsvorstand meinte, daß ein Arzt auch hierin nichts thun könne.

Eines Tages aber kam es unvermuthet an's Licht, weshalb der kleine Fritzi sich mit Nägeln und Zähnen gegen den Kindergarten gesträubt hatte.

Das Kind hatte sich vorgestellt, die Kinder dort in die Erde eingegraben, an Pfähle gebunden, mit Kalk bestrichen, mit Wasser und Tabakjauche begossen und an Nase und Ohren mittels einer großen Gartenscheere fleißig geputzt würden, wie er solches alles im Garten seines Vaters beobachtet hatte.

Konnte ein fühlendes Herz es der zarten Kindesseele verargen, wenn es vor einer solchen Behandlung in mimosenhafter Scheu zurückbebte?

Wir aber, als gewissenhafte und aufmerksame Menschenfreunde, wollen aus der Geschichte die Lehre ziehen, daß man die Kinder gar nicht früh genug mit den wahren Absichten Pestalozzi's und Fröbel's bekannt und vertraut machen kann. **BOS.**

Peter Bauer (München).

Vor'm Fenster

Blick' ich aus meinem niedrigen Haus
In Sommerszeiten zum Fenster hinaus,
Biege das Weinlaub ein wenig zur Seite,
Schweifen die Augen befeligt in's Weite.
Droben ein Bogen südöstlicher Himmel,
Unten der Obstgärten grünes Gewimmel,
Breit fließt der Lichtstrom von himmlischen
                                        Matten.
Golden verkropft er in tiefblauen Schatten.
Sommerluft, Blumenduft, Gesumm und Geflirr,
Fernhin verloren der Straßen Geschwirr.
Spatzen und Amseln auf schwankendem Aste,
Hell aus dem Grünen ein Fühnlein am Maste.
Kindliche Laute von üppigem Rasen,
Warnende Stimmen der Mütter und Basen.
Klappende Wäsche hängt zwischen den Wegen,
Und an den Büschen vor Beeren ein Segen.
Ueber dem allen ein kräftiger Odem,
Siedender Reife vollwürziger Brodem —
Alles ein Pulsschlag, ein Schwellen und Beben,
Kraftgesättigtes, zeugendes Leben.
So liegt das Gartenthal, lichtübergossen,
Fern erst, am Abhang, von Straßen umschlossen.
Dort auf der Höhe, mit flimmernden Scheiben
Hängt's wie ein Schloßbau hoch über dem
                                        Treiben.
Zu Sanct Johannis hat man es getauft, —
Darinnen das Alter im Stübchen sich kauft,
Wartend, bis anklopft mit knöchernem Finger
Der Heimwärtsrufer, der Friedenbringer.
Und ob da unten ein Lenzhauch thaut,
Ob lachender Sommerhimmel blaut,
Ob Herbstwind klagt, ob der Schnee blinkt im
                                        Thal,
Sie fragen dort oben: „zum letzten Mal?" —
Und weil ist's nicht zur letzten Reise —
Wo still ein Vogel zieht seine Kreise,
Lugt aus dem Grünen die Friedhofsmauer.
Es hängt eine Esche die Zweige in Trauer;
Die fließen wie düstere Bäche am Stamme.
Darüber flackert und glüht eine Flamme —
Die Sommersonne zündet sie helle
Am goldenen Kreuz der Todtenkapelle.
Das schmerzt die Augen, die gierig tranken —
Vor meinem Fenster nicken die Ranken.

Franz Langheinrich.

Integrated row ornament. Peter Bauer, 1897
Initials by Peter Behrens, 1908

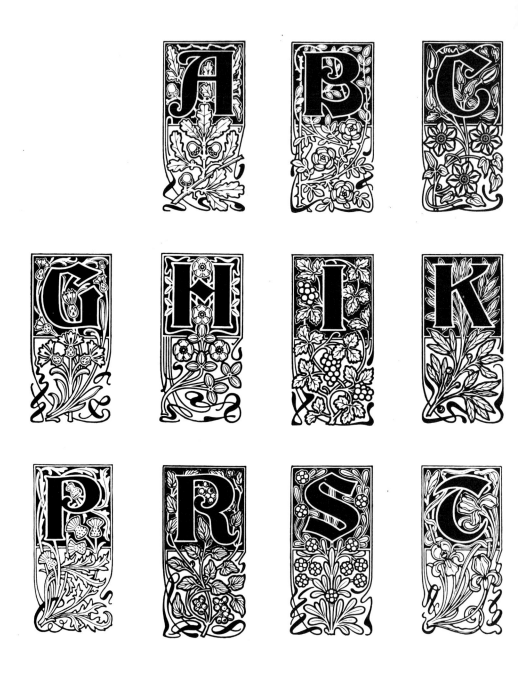

Plant initials in art nouveau style. Germany, 20th cn.

Plant initials in art nouveau style. Germany, 20th cn.

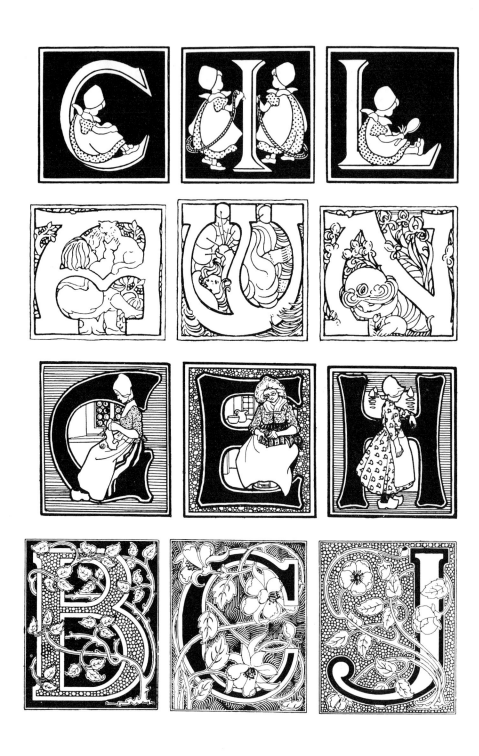

Figure initials by unknown artists, 1900

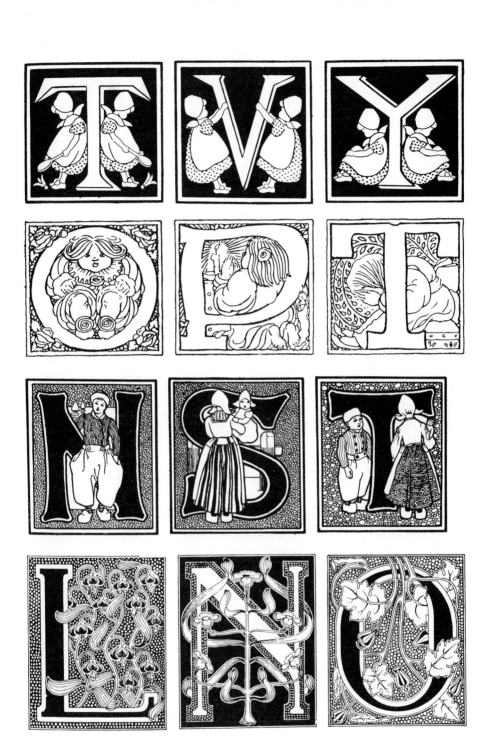

Figure initials by unknown artists, 1900

Initials by Heinrich Vogeler, beginning of the 20th cn. Executed by
Rudhardsche Gießerei, Offenbach

ALS Mr. Hiram B. Otis, der amerikanische Gesandte, Schloß Canterville kaufte, sagte ihm ein jeder, daß er sehr töricht daran täte, da dieses Schloß ohne Zweifel verwünscht sei.

Sogar Lord Canterville selbst, ein Mann von peinlichster Ehrlichkeit, hatte es als seine Pflicht betrachtet, diese Tatsache Mr. Otis mitzuteilen, bevor sie den Verkauf abschlossen.

„Wir haben selbst nicht in dem Schloß gewohnt," sagte Lord Canterville, „seit meine Großtante, die Herzogin-Mutter von Bolton, einst vor Schreck in Krämpfe verfiel, von denen sie sich nie wieder erholte, weil ein Skelett seine beiden Hände ihr auf die Schultern legte, als sie gerade beim Ankleiden war. Ich fühle mich verpflichtet, es Ihnen zu sagen, Mr. Otis, daß der Geist noch jetzt von verschiedenen Mitgliedern der Familie Canterville gesehen worden ist, sowie auch vom Geistlichen unserer Gemeinde, Hochwürden Augustus Dampier, der in King's College, Cambridge, den Doktor gemacht hat. Nach dem Malheur mit der Herzogin wollte keiner unserer Dienstboten mehr bei uns bleiben, und Lady Canterville konnte seitdem des Nachts häufig nicht mehr schlafen vor lauter unheimlichen Geräuschen, die vom Korridor und von der Bibliothek herkamen."

„Mylord," antwortete der Gesandte, „ich will die ganze

Fairy-tale illustrations by Heinrich Vogeler, beginning of the 20th cn.

Fairy-tale illustrations by Heinrich Vogeler, beginning of the 20th cn.

Fairy-tale illustrations by Heinrich Vogeler, beginning of the 20th cn.

Designs for the magazine "Pan" by Heinrich Vogeler, ca. 1900

Letters from the magazine "Pan" by Otto Eckmann, ca. 1900

Initials in art nouveau style (from top to bottom, from left to right): 1st row: anon., about 1902; W. Christie, 1905; anon., about 1900; 2nd row: anon., about 1900; N. Dominy, 1905; E. G. Hallam, 1905; 3rd row: H. G. Spooner, 1905; anon., about 1900; W. Christie, 1905; 4th row: anon., 1902; anon., 1902; anon., 1902

1st row: anon. 1903; E. G. Hallam, 1905; Ethel Larcombe, 1903; anon., 1902; 2nd row: W. Christie, 1905; anon., about 1900; anon., about 1902; 3rd row: H. G. Spooner, 1905; W. Gilliard, 1903; B. Tennant, 1903; 4th row: anon., about 1900; anon., about 1900; Paul Haustein, 1908

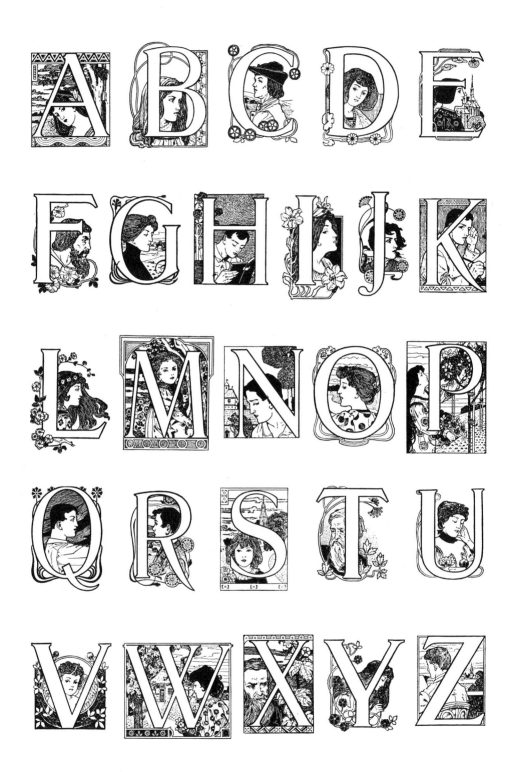

Initials in art nouveau style. Germany, beginning of the 20th cn.

Wood engravings by Karl Rössing, 1923

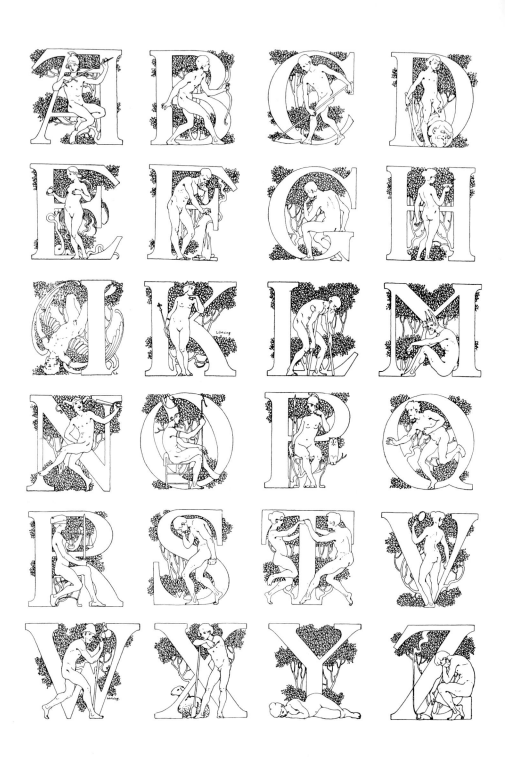

Decorative letters by Karl Lürtzing, 1908

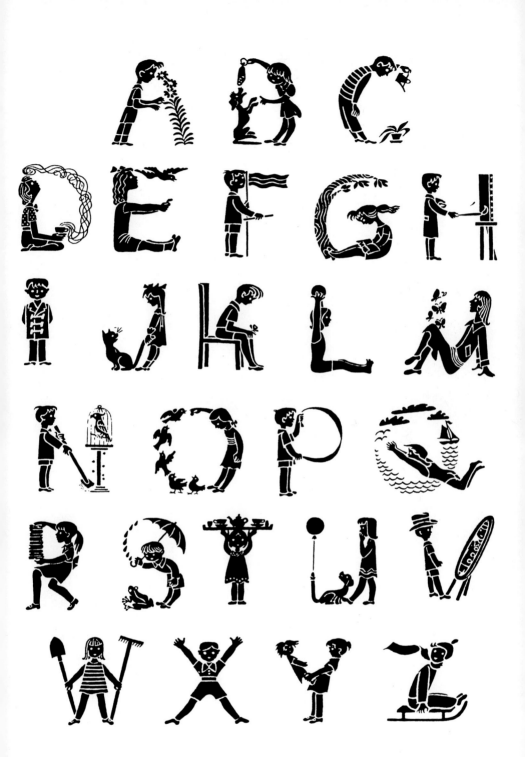

Children alphabet, about 1920

Surrealistic alphabet by Jindřich Heisler, about 1950

Surrealistic alphabet by Jindřich Heisler, about 1950

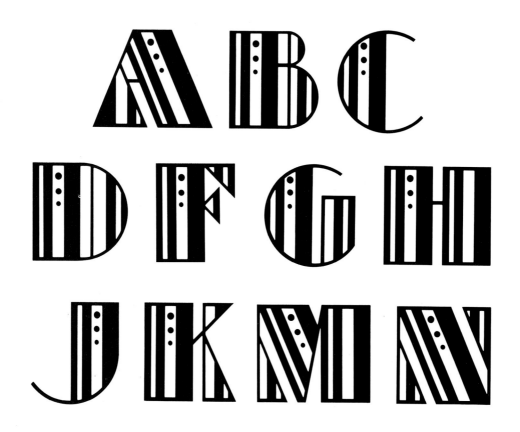

Alphabet in Art-Deco style by Marcia Loeb, 1972

Alphabet in Art-Deco style by Marcia Loeb, 1972

RAIN

ABCDE
KLMNO
UVW

Alphabet in Art-Deco style by Marcia Loeb, 1972

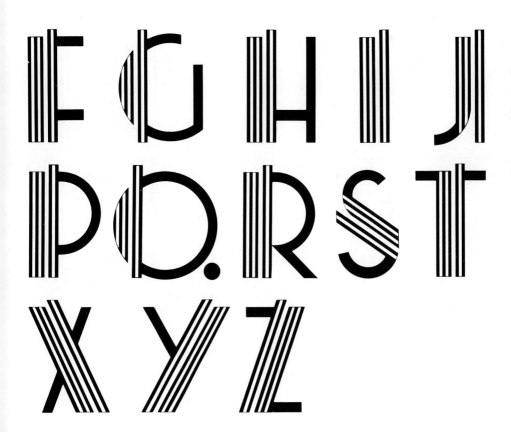

Alphabet in Art-Deco style by Marcia Loeb, 1972

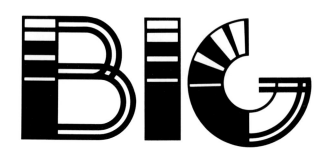

Alphabet in Art-Deco style by Marcia Loeb, 1972

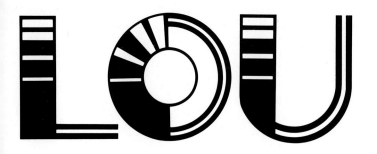

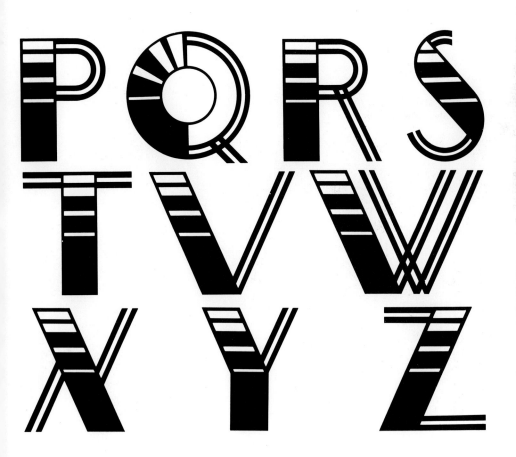

Alphabet in Art-Deco style by Marcia Loeb, 1972

267

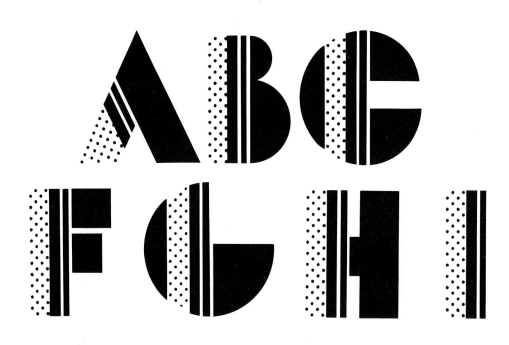

Alphabet in Art-Deco style by Marcia Loeb, 1972

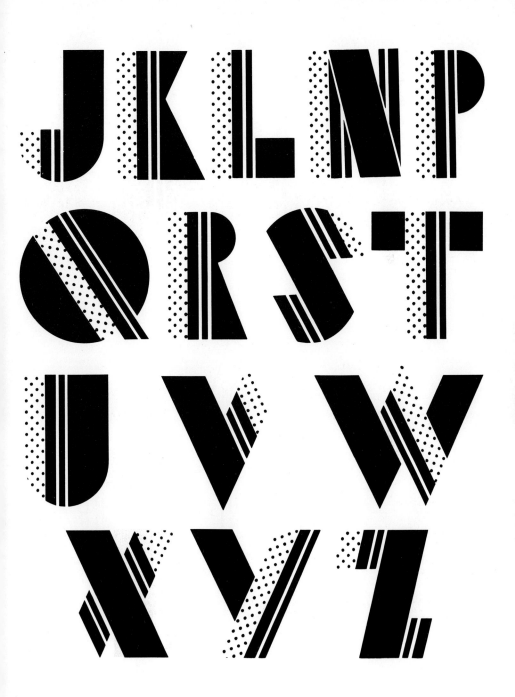

Alphabet in Art-Deco style by Marcia Loeb, 1972

Alphabet in Art-Deco style by Marcia Loeb, 1972

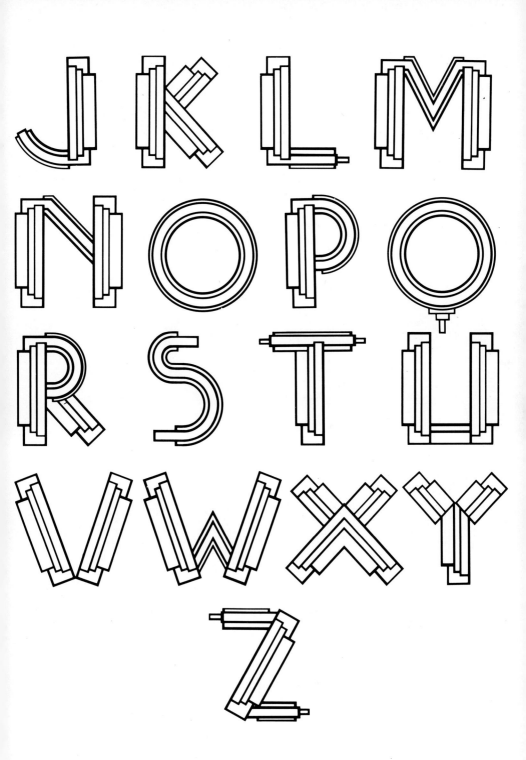

Alphabet in Art-Deco style by Marcia Loeb, 1972

ZIG

B C D D E

F H J K

L M N

Alphabet in Art-Deco style by Marcia Loeb, 1972

ZAG

OPQR

STUV

WXY

Alphabet in Art-Deco style by Marcia Loeb, 1972

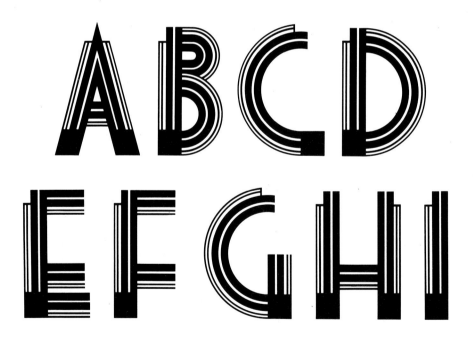

Alphabet in Art-Deco style by Marcia Loeb, 1972

Alphabet in Art-Deco style by Marcia Loeb, 1972

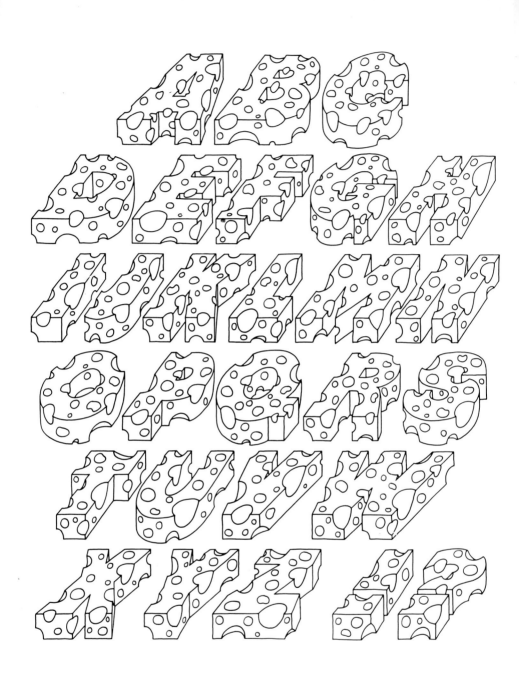

Pictorial letters by Jean Larcher, 1976

ONCE UPON A TIME A LITTLE MOUSE

Pictorial letters by Jean Larcher, 1976

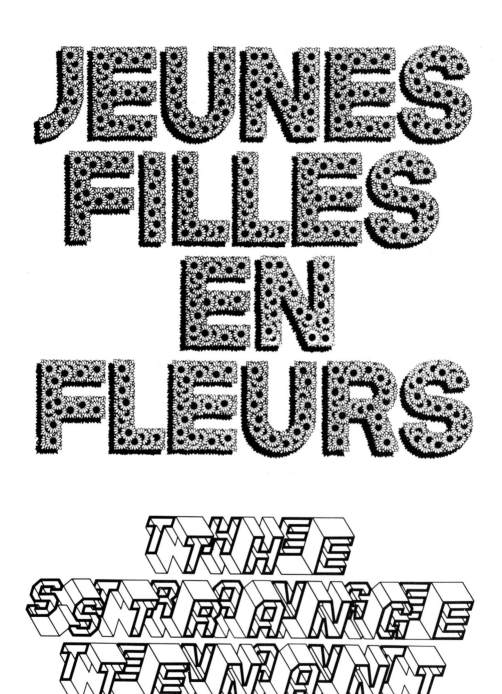

Pictorial letters by Jean Larcher, 1976

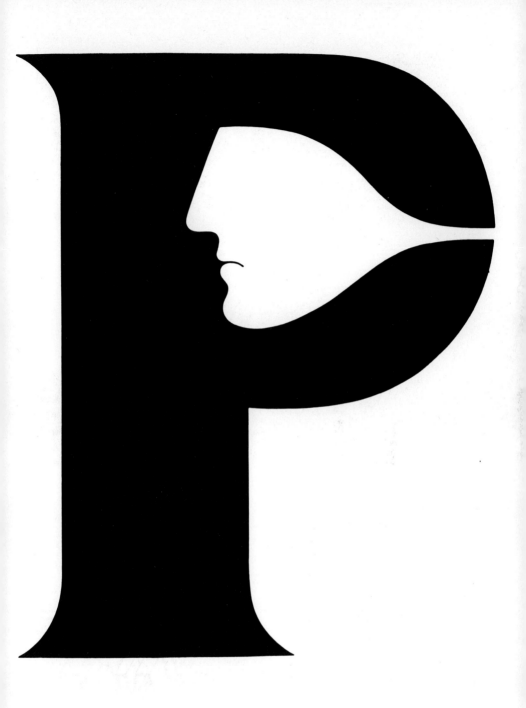

Pictorial letter by Lars Jonsson, 1981

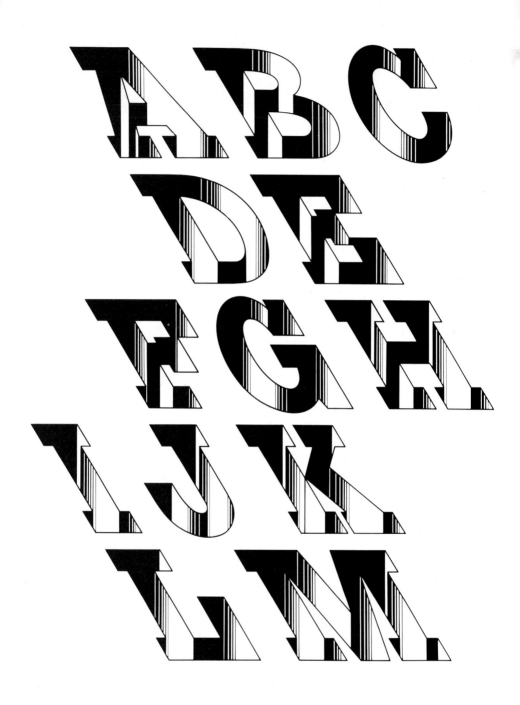

Pictorial letters by Jean Larcher, 1976

Pictorial letters by Jean Larcher, 1976

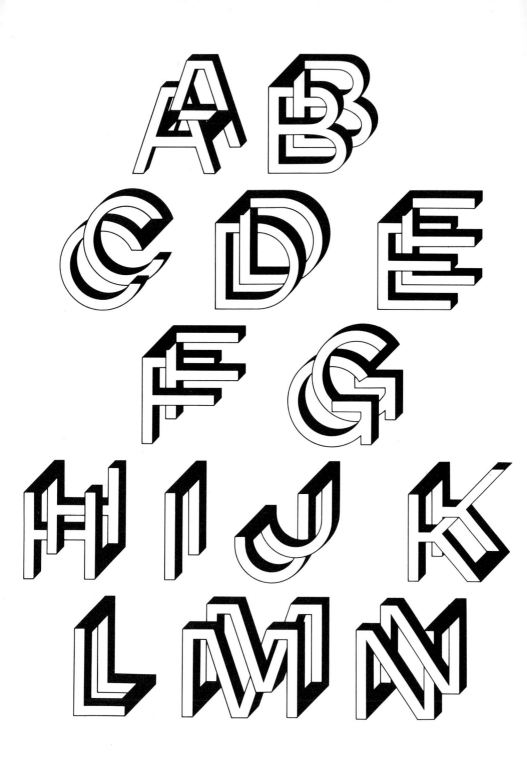

Pictorial letters by Jean Larcher, 1976

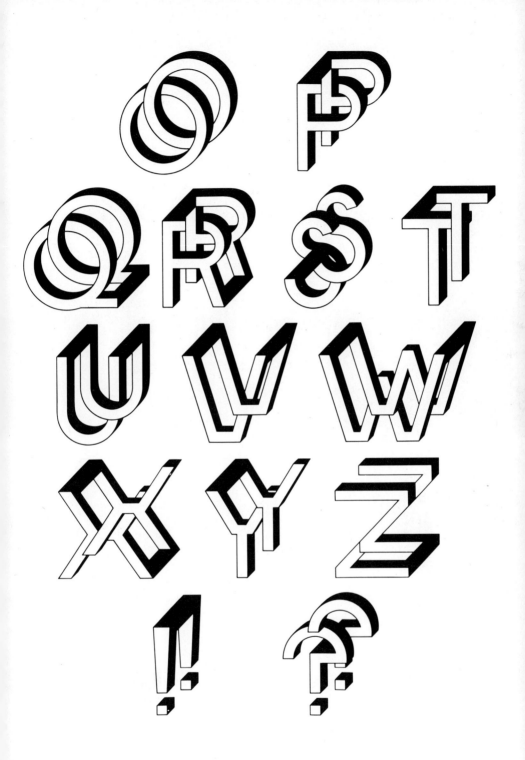

Pictorial letters by Jean Larcher, 1976

Pictorial letters by Jean Larcher, 1976

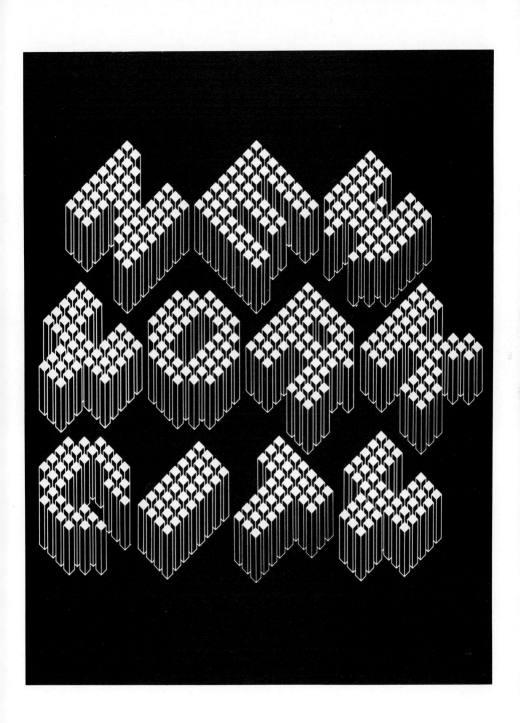

Pictorial letters by Jean Larcher, 1976

Pictorial letters by Jean Larcher, 1976

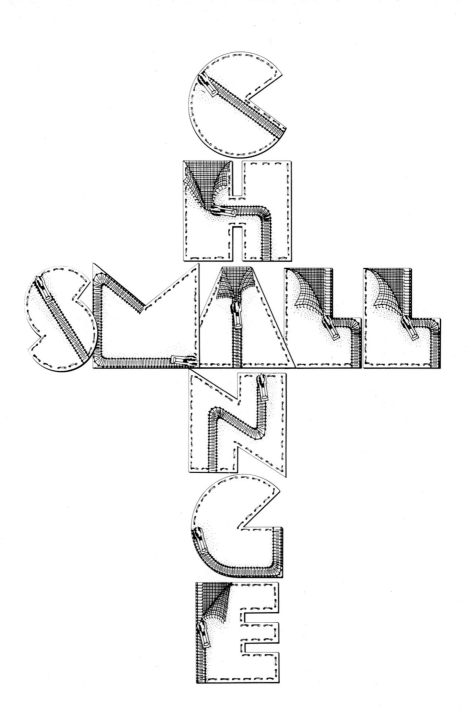

Pictorial letters by Jean Larcher, 1976

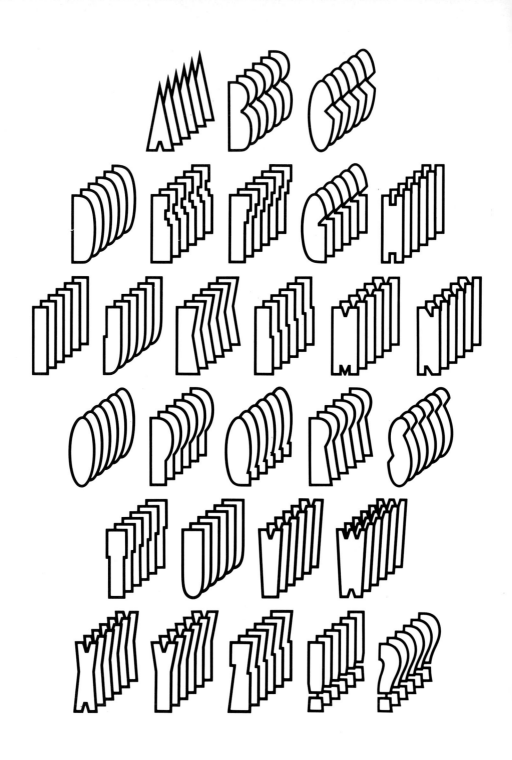

Pictorial letters by Jean Larcher, 1976

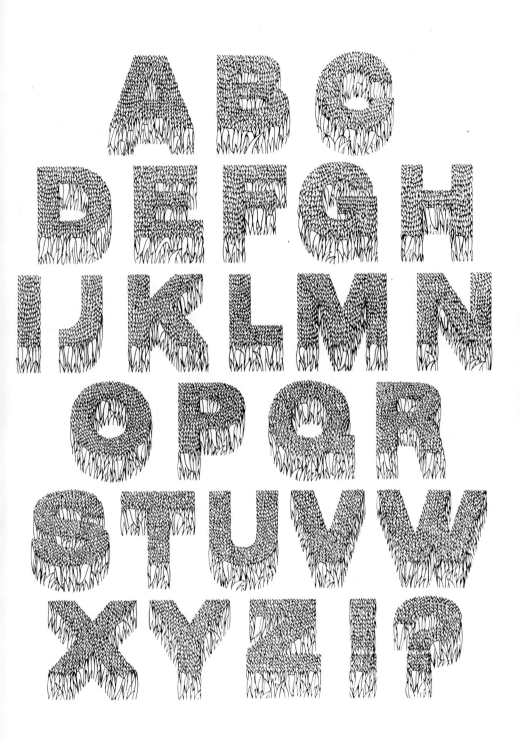

Pictorial letters by Jean Larcher, 1976

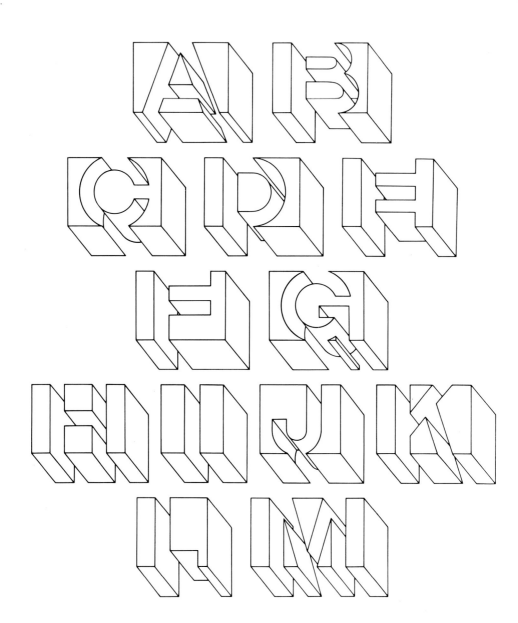

Pictorial letters by Jean Larcher, 1976

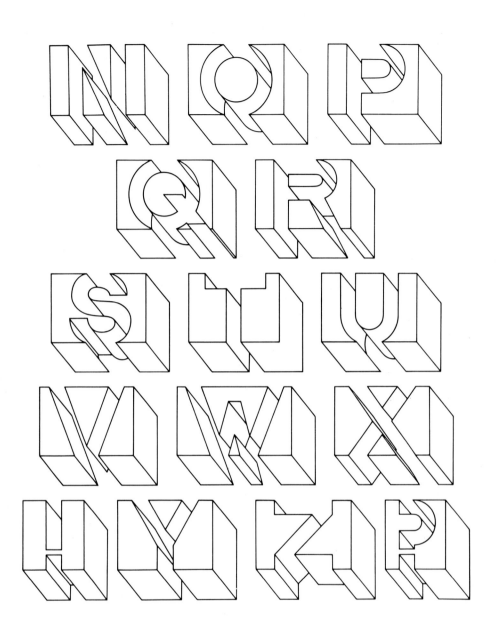

Pictorial letters by Jean Larcher, 1976

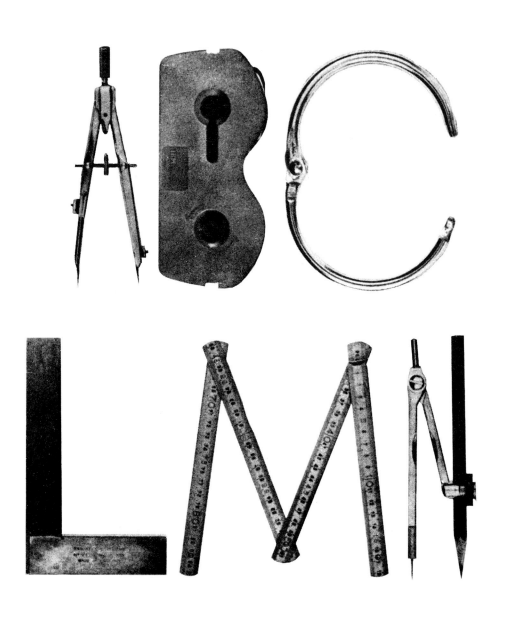

Decorative initials by Mervin Kurlansky, USA

Decorative initials by Mervin Kurlansky, USA

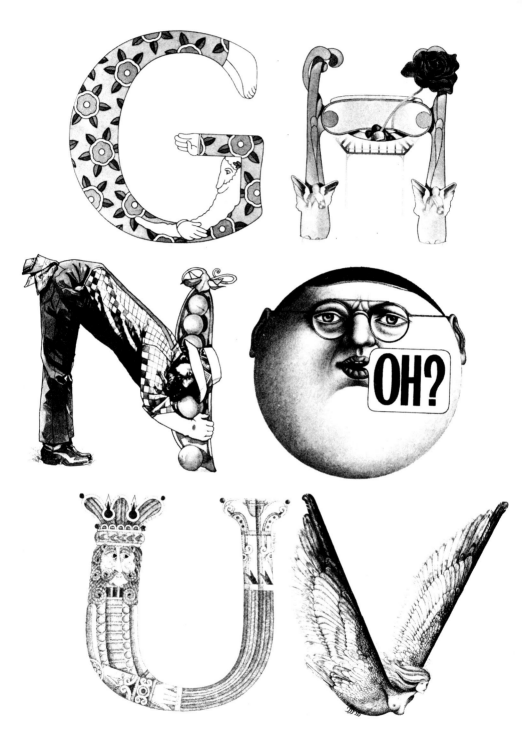

Decorative initials by various illustrators:
G = Milton Glaser, H = Bob Alcorn, N = Norman Green, O = Roy Carruthers,
U = Murray Tinkelman, V = Heather Cooper

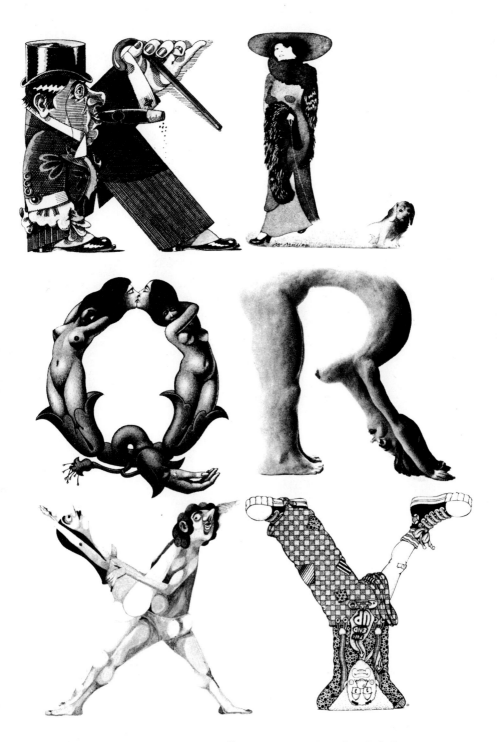

K = Gerry Gersten, L = Jim McMullen, Q = Roger Hane, R = Bob Grossman,
X = Jerome Snyder, Y = Marvin Mattelson

"Catphabet" by Jill Tannenbaum, USA

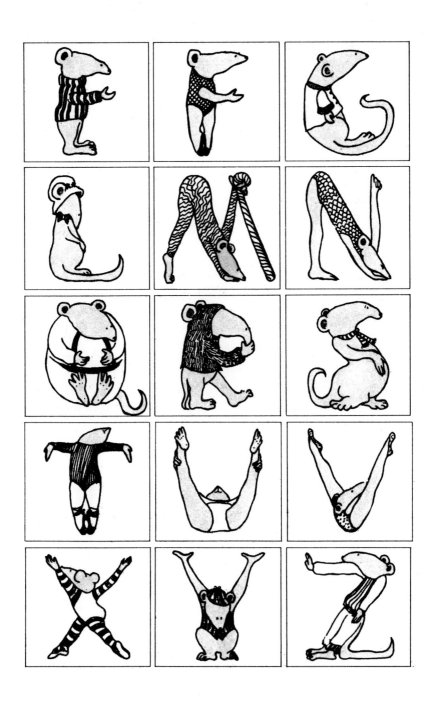

Figure alphabet by Nancy Schneider, USA

Cat alphabet by Debi Gardener, USA

Decorative letters by Klaus Bliesener, Germany

Surrealistic design by Mario Botas, Portugal

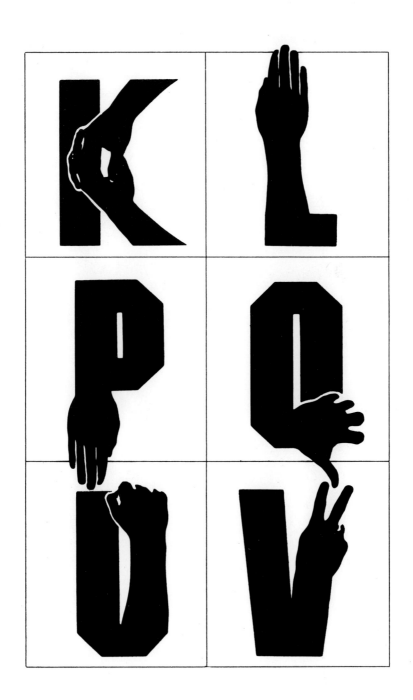

Hand-signal alphabet by Steven Bennett, USA

Cartoon-alphabet by Günther Hugo Magnus, Germany

Cartoon-alphabet by Günther Hugo Magnus, Germany

The "Coloring-in alphabet" by Jean Larcher, France

The "Coloring-in alphabet" by Jean Larcher, France

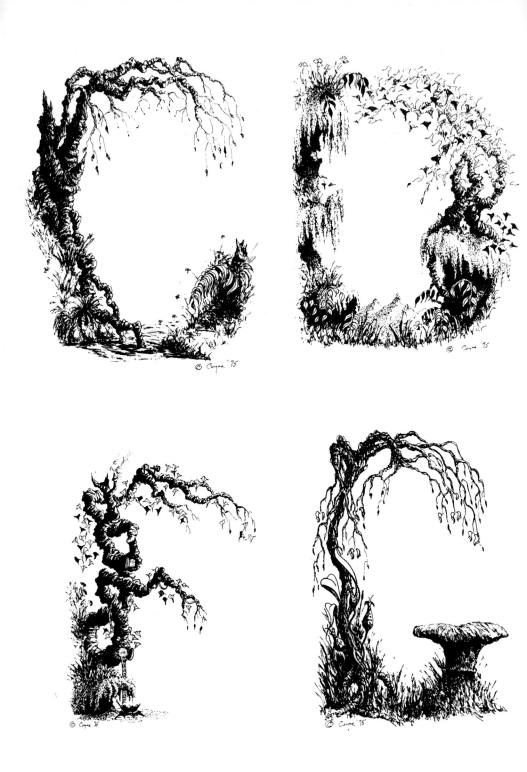

The "Living Alphabet" by Richard Coyne, USA

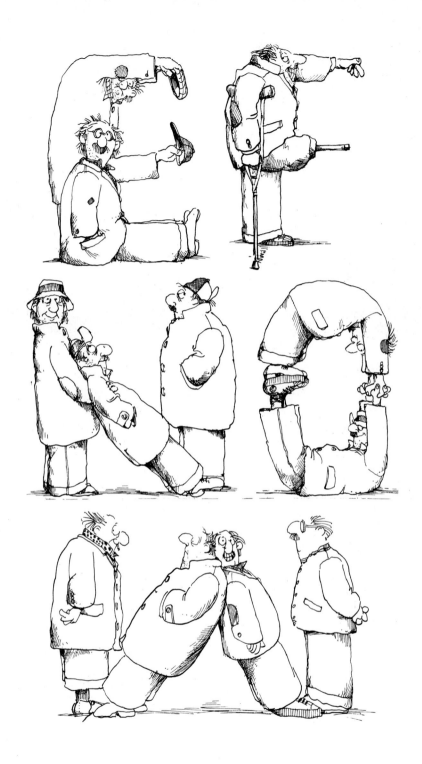

Design by John Caldwell, USA

Design by Lon Spiegelman, USA

Decorative letters by Paul Rounds Schiemer, USA

Design by Linda Bourke, USA

Design by Linda Bourke, USA

Decorative initials by various students of the School of Design at the Edinburgh College of Art

Decorative initials by various students of the School of Design at the Edinburgh College of Art

"Beastly alphabet" by Lynne Cherry, USA

"Beastly alphabet" by Lynne Cherry, USA

Cat alphabet (no indication)

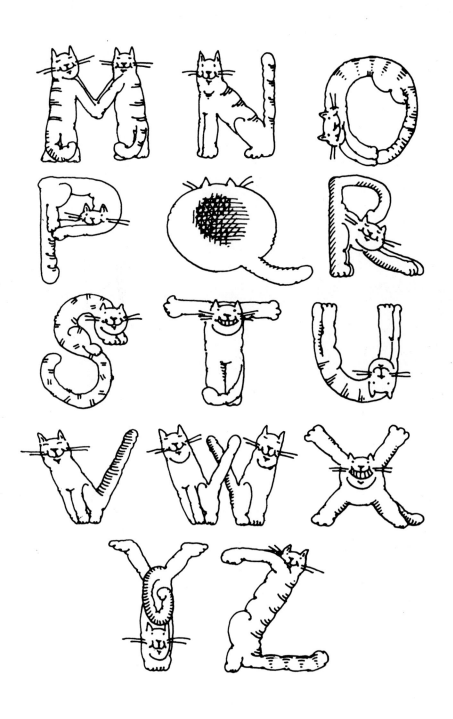

Cat alphabet (no indication)

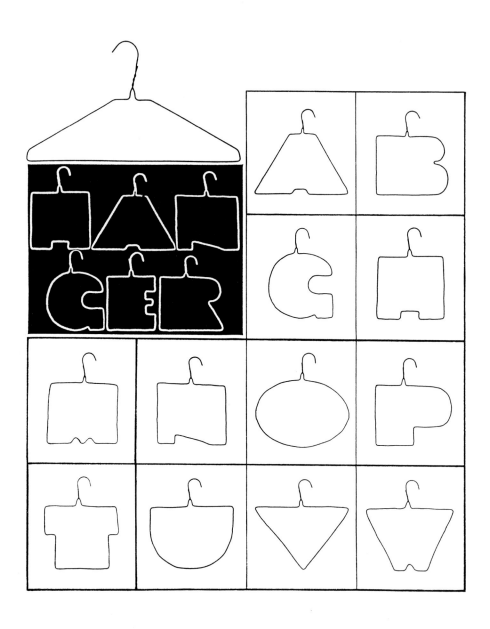

Wire alphabet by Conrad Jones, USA

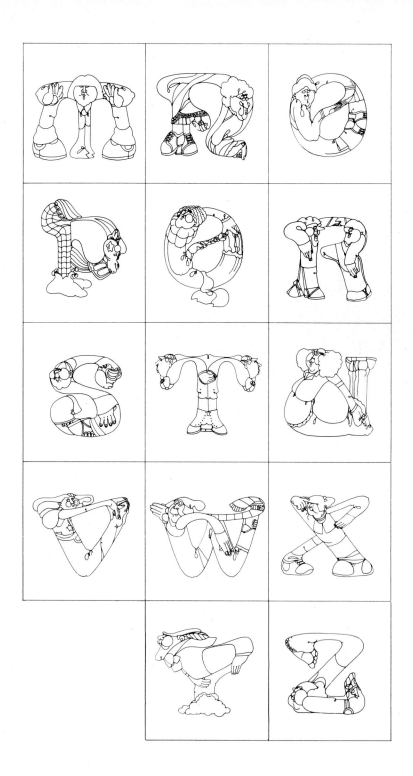

Comic alphabet by Denise Brunkus, USA

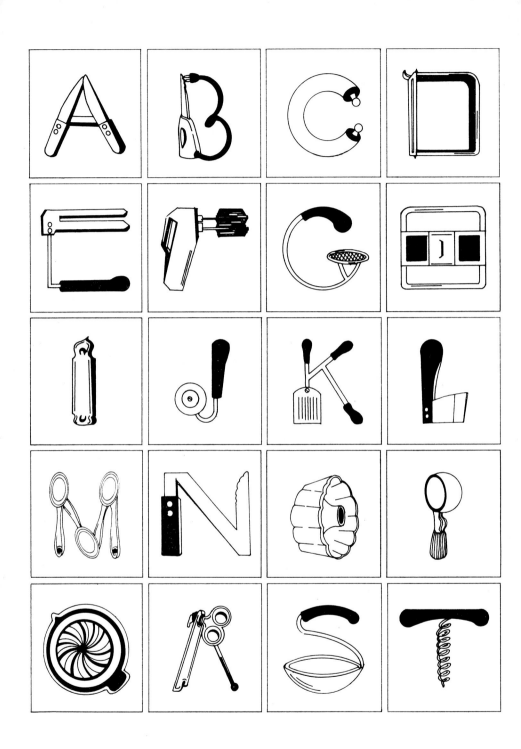

Utensil alphabet by Judy Carrsio, USA, 1979

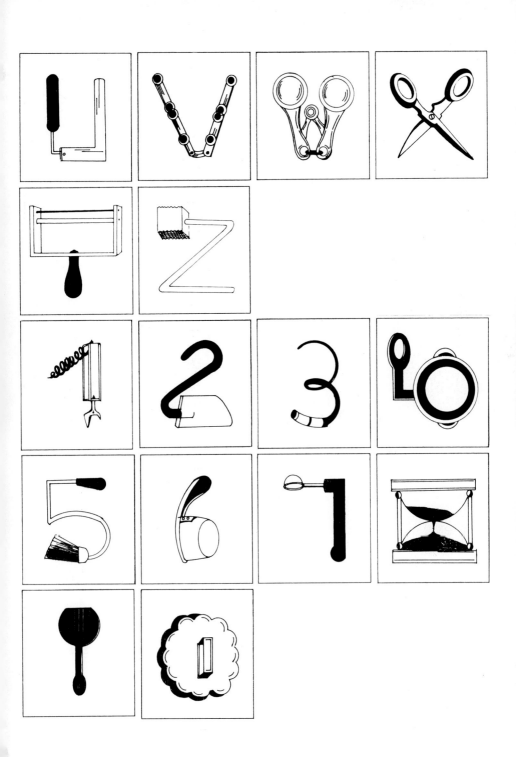

Utensil alphabet by Judy Carrsio, USA, 1979

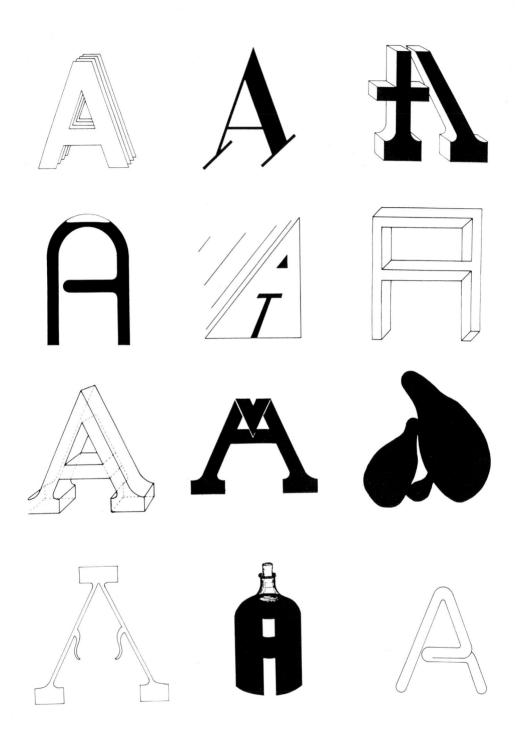

Studies from the Academy of Fine Arts, Brunswick, 1983

Studies from the Academy of Fine Arts, Brunswick, 1983

Studies from the Academy of Fine Arts, Brunswick, 1983

Studies from the Academy of Fine Arts, Brunswick, 1983

Studies from the Westend Art School, Frankfurt on Main, 1983

Studies from the Westend Art School, Frankfurt on Main, 1983

Studies from the Westend Art School, Frankfurt on Main, 1983

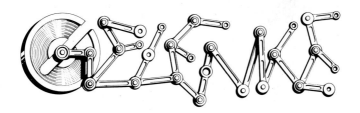

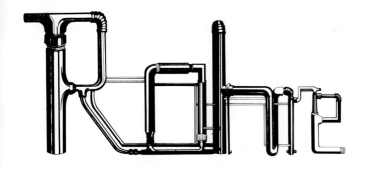

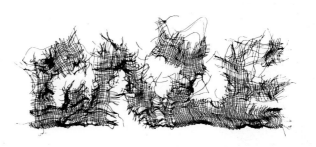

Studies from the Westend Art School, Frankfurt on Main, 1983

329

Studies from the Westend Art School, Frankfurt on Main, 1983

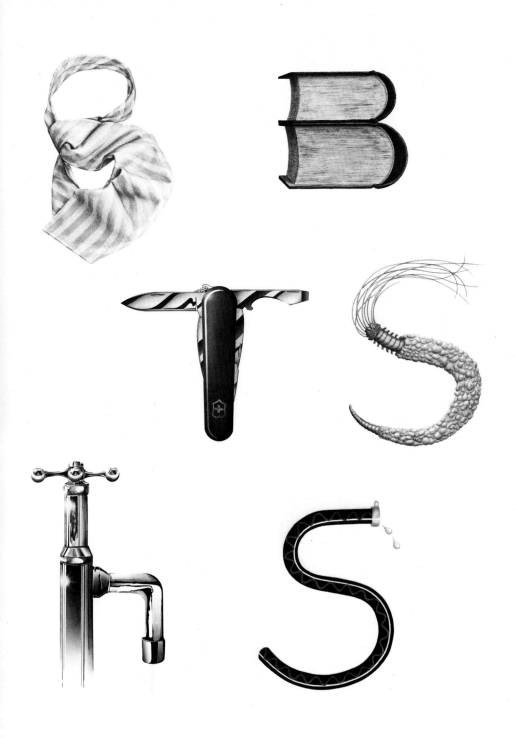

Studies from the Westend Art School, Frankfurt on Main, 1983

Studies from the Westend Art School, Frankfurt on Main, 1983

Studies from the Westend Art School, Frankfurt on Main, 1983

Sources

J. J. G. Alexander, Initialen aus großen Handschriften, Prestel Verlag, Munich 1978

Gustav Barthel, Konnte Adam schreiben? Weltgeschichte der Schrift. DuMont Schauberg, Cologne 1972

Carol Belanger Grafton, Bizarre and Ornamental Alphabets, Dover Publications, New York 1981

Carol Belanger Grafton, Historic Alphabets and Initials. Woodcut and Ornamental. Dover Publications, New York 1977

A. F. Butsch, Die Bücherornamentik der Renaissance, Hirth, Leipzig 1878

Hermann Degering, Die Schrift. Atlas der Schriftformen des Abendlandes vom Altertum bis zum Ausgang des 18. Jahrhunderts, Ernst Wasmuth, Berlin 1929

Florid and unusual alphabets by Midolle, Silvestre and Others, Dover Publications, New York 1976

Clarence P. Hornung, Handbook of early advertising art, Dover Publications, New York 1956

Albert Kapr, Deutsche Schriftkunst, VEB Verlag der Kunst, Dresden 1955

Jean Larcher, Phantastic Alphabets, Dover Publications, New York 1976

Marcia Loeb, New Art Deco Alphabets, Dover Publications, New York 1975

Alexander Nesbitt, Decorative Alphabets and Initials, Dover Publications, New York 1959

Novum Gebrauchsgraphik 7 and 9/1983, Munich

Michael Weisser, Ornament und Illustration um 1900, Dieter Fricke, Frankfurt on Main 1980

U&lc. International. The International Journal of Typographics, Ireland

Who's Who in Graphic Art, Vol. 2. Edited by Walter Amstutz. de Clivo Press, Dübendorf 1983